Also By Martha A. Aas

Pearls on a String: A Woman's Journey to the Past

Threads of Hope

Caring for Babies Across Three Continents

By

Martha Andrea Aas, M.D.

To Bebbie in memory
of the many years we
worked together.

Martha A. Aas

Published in the United States of America

ISBN 978-0-6158408-5-7
First Lakeberry Press Edition 2013
Library of Congress Control Number:

Cover by Marlene Wisuri

The characters in this book, whether babies or parents, are composite
figures and do not represent actual people. All locations in Minnesota
have been changed.

DEDICATION

This book is dedicated to all the nurses at the Neonatal Intensive Care Unit at St. Mary's Medical Center in Duluth, Minnesota and to retired nurse, Benoît Tindankir, Ngaoundéré, Cameroon.

We don't accomplish anything in this world alone…And whatever happens is the result of the whole tapestry of one's life and all the weavings of individual threads from one to another that creates some thing.

Sandra Day O'Connor

Prologue

Aden, Arabia

Without leaps of imagination, or dreaming, we lose the excitement of possibilities. Dreaming, after all, is a form of planning.

Gloria Steinem

Traveling through the searing desert of the British Protectorate of Aden, now part of the Republic of Yemen, I felt the sand crunching between my teeth as it poured in through the back of the Land Rover. My mouth was dry, and I longed to relieve my thirst with fresh clean water. A bath this morning in the Gulf of Aden had left my skin with a grayish layer of salt that now—with the addition of perspiration and dust—had morphed into sheets of brown residue. My khaki shorts and shirt were rumpled and sweaty. I looked forward to getting to where we would stay for the night. There I would have a shower: a bucket of water poured over my body.

The year was 1952 and I was on a trip up-country from Aden with my Danish missionary parents and my sister, Anna. The driver of the Land Rover—a 1950 Series 1 with three seats in front, two metal benches in the back, and a canvas cover—was Dr. Raymond Smith, a medical missionary. Cans of gasoline jostled around Anna's and my feet, fuel enough to get us back to Aden; the stench was over-powering. As we neared our destination of Gi'ar, the desert changed into a stark lava landscape; we were crossing the moon.

In Gi'ar Uncle Raymond—all our parents' colleagues were uncles or aunts to us missionary children—saw patients in the Mission Clinic, and as a Chief Medical Officer for the British government, he inspected standing water in the vicinity to make sure all mosquito larvae had been eradicated with DDT. We had lunch and quenched our thirst at the home of the Danish missionary nurses who ran the clinic. Then we continued into the interior of the Protectorate and arrived in the desert village of Mudia at sundown. We were housed in the British government fort, built of black lava stone and white mortar. It was a stronghold with parapets on top and loopholes through which soldiers could scan the countryside and defend Britain's honor during uprisings. I had my shower and bedded down that night on a military cot covered by a mosquito net. As I fell asleep I thought about the patients Uncle Raymond had seen that day.

I was in my fourteenth year and had been in Aden since age twelve. Here my parents spent a lifetime as missionaries, their residency interrupted only by home leaves every three to four years. Though I was conceived in Aden, I had not set foot on Arab soil until now, having spent the war years in Denmark, but I soon fell in love with the mystique of this place where my parents had worked since 1924. The Bedouins and their environment were part of the magic. I found a barren and enchanting beauty in the desert landscapes that surrounded us, and the Bedouins entranced me. They were hospitable and proud, and with their colorful *mushaddas* (head cloths), shirts, and *futahs* (loincloths), with the *gambiyyas* (two-edged daggers) at their waists and the guns across their shoulders, they were exotic warriors.

I had watched Uncle Raymond taking care of patients: malnourished women and children. Some had glassy eyes and rapid breathing and were in the throes of malaria attacks. Older children with eyes matted with infection stared at me: they had trachoma, an infectious disease that would eventually blind them if left untreated. Old men squatted along the walls. Women huge with pregnancy waited patiently. They were fearful at first, but as Uncle Raymond cared for them their fear changed to gratitude.

A year later our family spent a vacation month in Mukeiras, a town in the mountains of the interior of the British Protectorate. We visited villages where my father cared for people with skin ulcers, of which there were many. My father was an evangelizing missionary, but also had a nursing background. It fascinated me to see what simple wound care could do to heal these festering sores. Day after day we came back, and little by little the sores shrank, the skin healing from the periphery. This was momentous, I thought. With just a small amount of care, healing could be brought about and the skin restored.

After observing Uncle Raymond and my father in action I knew that I wanted to be a doctor and I wanted to work in this environment. I aimed to acquire the skills to treat patients like the ones they saw. I had no glory in mind, no sense of how I might make a lasting public health impact, no intent to build clinics or hospitals. All I wanted was to care for these people; not only because of their immediate and obvious needs, but also because of the way they marveled at the care they received, and their relief that death might not be imminent. Their gratitude made an impression on me, and though I could not have articulated it at the time, I somehow sensed that to be the recipient of that appreciation might give meaning to my life.

At the end of my father's term, when I was sixteen, I returned to Denmark. At age nineteen I started medical school. At that time all I knew was that I wanted to become a doctor, not what kind of doctor I wanted to be. If someone had asked me, I probably would have said a surgeon, only because Uncle Raymond was a surgeon.

Medical school turned out to be much different from what I had anticipated. I did not follow a straight line to the M.D. degree. I married and had two children during my studies. My husband, Hans, also a medical student, and I struggled to stay afloat, though we were greatly aided in our endeavors by the welfare state of Denmark. During those years, the dream of working in Aden was lost, for political as well as for personal reasons. Independence was the buzzword in the colonial world in the sixties and a year after I finished medical school in 1966, Aden became the independent People's Democratic Republic of Yemen, a socialist state. This set it on a rocky political course, at odds with its neighbor North Yemen, but in 1990 the two countries united into the Republic of Yemen. Still the country was by no means stable. Besides, with a husband and two children, my goals had shifted.

In a quest for further training, Hans and I came to the United States to intern in Kansas City, KS, but Denmark was still in our hearts and was where we wanted to spend our lives. So after one year we returned home. The rotating internship in Kansas City had given me more of a sense of the specialties within medicine. I liked both surgery and pediatrics. I did, however, have the feeling that a woman pediatrician might be more easily accepted than a woman surgeon.

When Denmark didn't provide the opportunities for further education we had hoped for, we returned to the U.S., this time to the Mayo Clinic in Rochester, Minnesota, where I had my pediatric training. At the end of three years of residency we returned to Denmark, which again proved to be a disappointment. Our home country did not accept our training, nor did professional growth there seem possible. We knew it was attainable in the U.S. and this led us to immigrate a year later, in 1973.

When I started medical school I could not have imagined the trajectory my life would take. Instead of leading to a developing country it led to the most developed, at least in some respects, country in the world. Instead of surgery it led to neonatology, a specialty that did not exist then, to a profession where I cared for the most vulnerable of patients: prematures and term newborns with problems. Instead of a solitary pursuit in medicine, it led to a partnership with my husband and the security of a family.

What eventually happened, late in my career, was even more surprising. I returned to a developing country to work there as a pediatrician/ neonatologist, not to Yemen which was still too unstable, but to Africa. As a seasoned doctor with much life experience behind me, I was less starry-eyed and more realistic, yet I was able in some sense to live out the dreams and desires of my youth to care for the poor and disadvantaged.

Though what follows is in part my story, it is especially the story of my patients, particularly the babies, I cared for: their often too early entry into this world, their triumphant lives and their sometimes tragic deaths. It is the story of the babies who left the deepest impressions on me, whether due to the environment into which they were born, or because of the circumstances of their births, their complicated early lives, their fights for survival, or their deaths. The babies I can't forget.

I. Becoming a Doctor

"Every man's life is a fairy tale, written by God's fingers."

Hans Christian Andersen

1. Less than Human

To love means loving the unlovable. To forgive means pardoning the unpardonable. Faith means believing the unbelievable. Hope means hoping when everything seems hopeless.

G.K. Chesterton

One day in 2012 while driving into Duluth from my home in Lakewood Township, I listened to *Talk of the Nation* on National Public Radio. I heard Neal Conan say something that catapulted me back in time:

"Looking back on atrocities he committed against the Chinese in Nanjing, a Japanese war veteran said, 'If I had thought of them as human beings I couldn't have done it, but I thought of them as animals, or below human beings.'"

"Sadly, history is full of such stories," Neal Conan reminded his listeners. He then went on to introduce the author David Livingstone Smith whose book, *Less Than Human: Why We Demean, Enslave and Exterminate Others* was to be discussed. As I listened I realized how aptly Smith's title describes the contents of the book and its frightening look at aspects of human thought, especially as played out during the many genocides of history.

My thoughts went back fifty-five years to a different time and place—to a place of such tranquility that atrocities were unthinkable. The place was the small provincial town of Dianalund in Denmark. Here one doctor, at the turn of the twentieth century, started what was to become a large epileptic hospital, *Kolonien Filadelfia*. By the mid to late 1950s it covered hundreds of acres of verdant farmland and had become a town of its own, with a church, stores, and numerous hospital wards where patients with intractable epilepsy or developmental handicaps were treated and cared for.

The Children's Hospital at *Kolonien Filadelfia* was nestled in the woods surrounding Dianalund. In the late fifties this one-storied complex was new, and was a comforting and bright place to work. At the time I was studying at the University of Aarhus and had three months off during the summers. As I had been enrolled at the Faculty of Medicine at the university since graduating from the *gymnasium* and planned to become a doctor, it seemed appropriate that I acquire some experience in dealing with patients. I got a job at this children's hospital as a substitute nurse's aide.

The hospital treated young patients with a variety of severe seizure disorders and also was a repository for children with severe developmental problems. My job was to be a caregiver and playmate. Neither role was natural to me at the time. I was the fourth child in a family of five and had spent no time around young children and had, in fact, never been a babysitter.

Yet I was not particularly distressed to discover I would be working in the section that housed those less than one year old. I was twenty and had spent three years catching up on my education after returning from Yemen. I was acutely aware that my practical skills were nonexistent, but I put my trust in my ability to learn.

As it turned out, nothing was as simple as I had thought. I found that changing diapers was an art. This was the era of cloth diapers. A cloth diaper in Denmark at the time was a two-by-two foot square of loosely-woven cotton cloth that one folded on the diagonal into a triangle and wrapped around the baby in a particular fashion. A pair of pants was slipped over to hold the diaper in place. Plastic diaper pants were either not discovered yet, or discouraged, as they prevented the caregiver from knowing when the diaper was wet and in need of replacing. To me it all sounded simple, but I quickly learned that a squirming child could make the task of changing diapers very difficult, and that a certain deftness was required.

Feeding babies also seemed simple. The milk—not formula as there were no formulas in Denmark then—was prepared in the kitchen, poured into bottles, and carried to the ward in wire baskets, the bottle openings covered with cardboard lids. In those days the caregiver had to slip the sterilized nipple onto the bottleneck; the screw lid holding the nipple in place was yet to be invented. Talk about a recipe for disaster! In the beginning I spilled half the milk before I managed to slide on the nipple. These practical considerations were only the tip of the iceberg however. Changing and feeding the actual patient was the real difficulty.

One particular child, Helle, became my nemesis and almost derailed my plans for the future. I don't know that I ever knew her diagnosis, yet the memory of this child is still vivid in my mind fifty-five years later. Helle was about ten months old, had carrot-red hair that stood straight up, was microcephalic and very spastic i.e. her muscles were tight and her extremities and body stiff. Furthermore, she screamed constantly, her body arched, her head thrown back. Periodically, she had generalized seizures and was probably on medication for this, but that was the concern of the nurses. My job was to report the seizures, and otherwise to take care of her: bathe her, clothe her, feed her, and settle her down when it was time for sleep. I quickly found that I failed miserably on all counts.

Diapering her was difficult because of the tightness of all her muscles, and because of her general irritability. When I had my own children, I found that a normal child of ten months already has learned the cues to cooperate in whatever will make the task easy and quick, but not so with Helle.

As any occupational therapist today will tell you, skill in facilitating bottle-feeding is paramount when dealing with a child with handicaps, but I was blissfully unaware of that then. I spent hours bottling and feeding her. She and I and our surroundings were a complete mess by the time we finished. Playing with her was out of the question. It was obvious even to me—at that uninformed stage of my life in medicine—that Helle was profoundly physically and mentally handicapped, unable to learn, and in need of custodial care only.

My frustration was intense as I tried to find something about this child that was engaging. There was nothing. I yearned for her nap times when I could forget about her for a while, but my attempts to settle her down for sleep were usually unsuccessful. I ended up putting her to bed, making sure she was unable to hurt herself, and then leaving her to scream. I remember her screaming as constant, but maybe it wasn't. Maybe it was just insistent enough to give me a memory of her constancy in letting the world know of her misery.

As I was an untrained worker at the time, with no medical background, I can make no judgment about whether she was provided with the appropriate treatment. I have no memory of her receiving physical therapy, though I would have to assume she did, as physical therapy was a heavily involved discipline at the institution. Of course she was not my only patient, but the one who took most of my time, the one I remember.

After trying for some time to find something to like about this child and finding nothing, I became aware that I couldn't stand her, that I literally hated her. This caused me enormous guilt. How could I hate a young innocent child, and what did harboring such feelings say about me as a person? As I struggled with this I became very concerned that I might lose my patience with her and become abusive toward her. These thoughts eventually caused me such distress that I sought out the psychiatrist who had treated me the year before for depression. I asked him how I could possibly become a physician when I could feel such anger toward a patient, to the point where I was afraid I might hurt her. He made me realize that my feelings were not unusual. The important thing was that I didn't act on them. He suggested that I ask to be assigned to another patient. I don't remember what happened thereafter. My conversation with the psychiatrist had obviously calmed me down and the rest of my experience at the children's hospital does not stand out in my memory.

For days after listening to Neal Conan's interview with the author of *Less than Human,* I kept thinking of my experience with Helle. I thought of the importance of always seeing the humanity in others. With my little patient it was difficult because she seemed to have no soul. There was nothing in her eyes that told me her mind was alive. Her body fought me every step of the way; she could not relax and mold her body to mine. There was no laughter. She was, however, in a human body, a body that had been destroyed by whichever disaster had happened in her development and she deserved all the love I could give her, or at least caring interaction.

I thought I might have learned then to accept a human being in any form, but as I came to care for sick babies, I continued to have the most trouble caring about the ones whose minds were destroyed. They tended to be mere objects to me and not persons, and I could rarely care deeply for them.

Yet, I think now that I can sense how easy it is to find oneself on a slippery slope and arrive at a justification for denying care or even life for such a person, especially if you lose sight of his or her human aspects.

Over the years these are thoughts I have tended to sweep under the carpet and ignore. Neal Conan's discussion made me revisit this issue, but doing so failed to resolve my feelings.

It was a huge eye-opener, however, to read Ian Brown's *The Boy in the Moon*. Ian Brown is an author and a feature writer for the newspaper *The Globe and Mail* in Canada. He and his wife have a child with the very rare condition: cardio-facio-cutaneous syndrome (CFC). He relates that physicians often try to be understanding and reassuring by saying, "I understand what you are going through." Ian Brown's message is that there is no way we can understand the hell that was his family's life for the decade they cared for their son. The boy had the intellectual capacity of an eighteen-month-old, couldn't eat (was fed through a gastric tube), had poor fine and gross motor skills, continued spells of crying, repeated infections, and eventually seizures. "Only if we have taken that journey ourselves, can we understand what parents of severely disabled children go through," says Ian Brown.

No physician understands a child's illness like his parents. They become the experts and the ultimate advocates for their children. When later as a neonatologist I discharged children with significant disabilities, I always made sure the parents were aware of this, but Ian Brown made me understand the truth of it to a much greater degree.

Parents of other CFC children tell Ian Brown that while their pediatricians offer them little in the form of solace, they are always curious and interested, something the parents don't necessarily value: to them it seems the physicians are only satisfying their curiosity, and that to them the severely disabled child is just a specimen.

To that I would say: Yes, physicians are and should be curious, curiosity drives their diagnosing of illnesses and their desire to keep up on the latest technologies and treatments. They also want to learn about the very rare syndrome confronting them. Since the parents are more knowledgeable than their physicians about their child's illness, this presents an opportunity for families to teach their doctor about their child. Physicians' jobs are to heal, but they feel helpless knowing they have no means to cure the special child in front of them, so they grab onto what they can offer, namely to treat the ear infection or whatever may temporarily be afflicting the child.

Do the physicians look at the children as specimens? It may seem that way, because they may be unable to acknowledge their insecurity. They know next to nothing about the particular rare syndromes in front of them and know even less about what it really means to care for a disabled child day in and day out.

Sometimes there are huge gaps in people's abilities to understand each other. It may be almost impossible to bridge such gaps, but what we can do is listen to people who have first-hand experience, like Ian Brown, and allow ourselves to become humbled as we stand in awe of what some parents are able to do for their vulnerable children.

Helle had provided me, a very young woman who was just beginning her life in medicine, with a small glimpse into the world of such children and their families.

2. Denmark

In 1959, I met and fell in love with my husband, Hans, a fellow medical student. I soon became pregnant with our son Michael. Having a child while still in medical school was a challenge, but with Hans's support and encouragement I continued my studies. Our medical school class was about 40 percent female and many students were married, some with children, so our situation was not unusual.

In Denmark, medical school is begun immediately after graduation from the *gymnasium* (high school). Our first four years were occupied with basic sciences. The academic year consisted of a fall and a spring semester, each of three months duration. There were no tests or exams until the last two months of the four years when tests were given in all the basic sciences in one grueling finale.

During the next four (clinical) years we had various rotations at the university hospitals, but because of the large breaks between semesters, and because of a shortage of physicians in Denmark, many medical students also spent some of their free months working as substitute physician at county hospitals.

My first clinical rotation was in internal medicine at Aarhus Municipal Hospital. One of my morning duties was lab work, done in a small lab right on the floor. I did simple tests like the hematocrit, the counting of red blood cells, and the counting and differentiation of white blood cells. I examined urine samples and stool samples. The latter were in the lab when I arrived, but I had to draw the blood myself. The purpose of medical students doing these labs was for us to become proficient in how to perform simple lab tests, so that if in the future we should find ourselves in a small hospital where a lab technician was not at our beck and call, we would know how to do these tests. No one demonstrated them for us. There were written instructions hanging on the walls, so it was just a matter of following instructions.

On rounds with the professor, medical students—whether male or female—were often made to look foolish. We were lowest on the totem pole with second and first registrars ranking above us, but we were the ones asked the most questions. Afraid of making a fool of yourself in front of the professor and your soon-to-be colleagues, it was easy to feel intimidated. This bullying appeared inherent to the system and I assume the professor himself had been exposed to it as a medical student. Similarly, if the professor questioned the lab test I had done, he would ask, "Do you really know what you are doing? Would you please go back and do it over?" You had to have a broad back to survive this.

During the summer of 1963, I spent three months as a substitute physician at a small municipal hospital in Kalundborg. Hans was serving part of his military duty in boot camp during that time. I had chosen Kalundborg Hospital because Hans's brother-in-law, Johs, was on the surgical staff there. His wife, Hans's sister Karen, cared for our son Michael when I worked or was on-call. This was good for Michael, as he got to know his cousins well.

I found it very exciting to finally be intimately involved in caring for patients. In minor surgery I learned by following the old adage: *see one, do one, teach one.* I didn't get to do much teaching, but Johs started by showing me how to do a procedure. Later, I did the same procedure under his supervision, and then I was confident to be on my own. Johs was interested in obstetrics and gynecology (he would eventually become an ob-gyn resident in Kansas City), and with his help and the help of the midwives at the hospital, I learned how to handle uncomplicated deliveries and to identify problems occurring during labor.

Midwifery has a long history in Denmark. Centuries ago there were only lay midwives, but in the sixteenth century midwifery was established as a guild with an apprenticeship followed by an exam. In the seventeenth century midwives were required to have been taught and examined by an, of course male, physician. When birth hospitals were established in the nineteenth century, all teaching of midwives took place there. For centuries midwives have been part of and are still integral to maternal-infant care in Denmark and are responsible for all uncomplicated prenatal and perinatal care. Some midwives are on the staff at hospitals where deliveries take place and others are in private practice.

I greatly enjoyed my time at Kalundborg Hospital as I worked in all areas: made rounds and saw patients on the medical floor, assisted at surgeries and deliveries, and saw and treated patients in the emergency room. At night I had to do the simple lab work myself and felt well prepared after my experience in the internal medicine department in Aarhus.

My clinical rotation at the birth hospital at Aarhus University was much more pleasant than my first rotation, the one in internal medicine. The atmosphere was welcoming, the registrars were interested in teaching, and we learned much from them. We were actively involved in deliveries and took call. The student call rooms were up under the eaves of the hospital roof. We each had our own small room at the periphery of a large sitting area. There were probably six to eight students on the service at one time and when we were not busy we would share stories and experiences. Whenever a patient was admitted during the evening or night, we were called in turn to take the history and do the initial exam before the midwife appeared. If we got along well with the midwife she would let us manage the delivery with her looking over our shoulder. By that time I had already had some experience delivering babies, as had most of the other students, and we were given more responsibility than on other services.

We had decided to have a party on the last night our group of students was on call. Everyone had brought food to share as well as wine. That night was relatively quiet, but we decided beforehand that if a patient were admitted two of us would go down, help each other take the patient's history and do the exam, write everything up and we could be back in no time. The vaingloriousness of youth!

A patient was admitted and Morten Kraft and I went down to the patient's room. Morten introduced himself as Dr. Kraft and me as his assistant. While Morten took the history, I sat on a stool in a corner, pen and paper at the ready, taking notes. I wore a surgical mask so the patient would not smell wine on my breath. The only problem was that I found the situation so hilarious that I was about to crack up with laughter. With my shoulders shaking and not paying enough attention, I kept asking Morten to repeat himself, barely refraining from laughing out loud.

I also wanted to tell him, "Maybe you should ask about this…or that…" but felt that would give the show away. What the patient was thinking nobody asked, but she must have been mystified. Respect for patients had not been inculcated in us.

Our clinical years ended with another marathon of exams. During December and January, the months of our exams, our now two sons Michael and Peter went to their grandparents' homes. We had oral exams every three to four days. After we had finished one huge tome of a textbook and its attendant exam, it was on to the next: internal medicine, surgery, pharmacology, pathology, microbiology, statistics, forensic medicine, and others that I no longer recall.

Forensic medicine was our last exam, and with a last name starting with the ultimate letter in the Danish alphabet (Aa=Å), Hans and I were the very last students to be examined. I vividly remember my proud mother and father in the audience, having been allowed to audit my exam. I was given the case of a sailor who during the cold winter was found dead on the deck of his ship in Aarhus Harbor. What did he die from? It was an easy, open and shut case.

Afterwards, our extended family assembled outside the examining room. Michael, five and a half years old, was jumping up and down shouting, "We're done! We're done!" Peter at only eighteen months didn't know what all the hoopla was about, but was happy to be back in his father and mother's arms. Both boys had in fact participated in this marathon by being yanked out of their routines.

We left school without debt, as tuition at the university was free. The idea was of course that we would eventually pay back to society, in the form of taxes, what it had expended on us. Since we had very little income during our studies, the state had also provided free childcare of excellent quality.

Despite some deficiencies, the Danish medical education system was excellent in that it put great demands on students to study independently to acquire all the knowledge needed to be a doctor, at the same time giving them plenty of opportunities for clinical experience.

As the U.S. was experiencing its own shortage of American interns, the private Swedish hospital Trinity Lutheran in Kansas City, Kansas had turned to recruiting interns among Danish medical graduates. We decided to apply for our internship at that institution. The Danish doctors who applied were fluent in English, self-motivated, and well qualified as they had gained significant clinical experience working as substitute physicians. Hans and I considered an internship in the United States a light-hearted adventure, well deserved after the intense studies of medical school, and an attractive way to get to know the United States. In preparation, we had passed the test given by the Educational Commission for Foreign Medical Graduates (ECFMG) the year before.

During our internship we had a rotation at Children's Mercy Hospital in Kansas City, Missouri. I would treasure my time there. This was my first exposure to an African-American population whose idiomatic speech I barely understood. I found that I loved working with children and was fascinated by their diseases, different as they are from those of adults.

As I think back to that time I realize that in the mid 1960s, American public institutions—Kansas City Children's and Kansas City General Hospital included—were much like hospitals in the developing world: the examining tables in the emergency rooms were made from crude four-by-fours, painted in garish colors, with thin vinyl covered mattresses that could be easily wiped down. The bed linen had seen better days; one suspected it had started its life in private hospitals. Coming from the fastidious modern welfare state of Denmark, we were astounded that this was the best the public system in the wealthy U.S. could offer. But whereas the facilities left much to be desired, the medical care and teaching were top-notch. Daily we made rounds with the Chief of the Hospital, Dr. Stan Hellerstein, a kind and gentle man, who taught me much, and who eventually was responsible for my choice of specialty.

When on call at Children's, interns and residents slept in bunk beds, in one room. I expected to sleep there, but that was not deemed appropriate. Women interns slept in the nurses' dorm. The room there had no phone, but I was promised that a guard would get me when the hospital needed me. This became a vexing problem. Though I was happy not to have to sleep in a non-air-conditioned room surrounded by sweaty, snoring male bodies, I soon realized that I missed out on learning experiences. I wasn't called often enough, because no one thought to call the guard in time to get me there. Consequently I decided to stick around in the ER until late at night.

Having come from a country where women medical students were almost half of the student body, I was used to being treated on an equal footing with the men. In the U.S., on the other hand, only 5% of medical students at this time were female. In Kansas City I encountered an attitude to women doctors that was at once patronizing and protective, mostly out of uncertainty of how to deal with us.

At the end of our internship we returned to Denmark, to the town of Viborg, where Hans served his military duty as an officer in the Danish army, at the same time working as second registrar at a psychiatric hospital and later at a rehab center. Meanwhile I spent a year in radiology—half of it while I was pregnant—doing procedures such as upper G-Is and barium enemas. I also did pneumoencephalograms, a terrifying, outdated procedure that involves injecting air into the central nervous system through a spinal needle inserted in the lumbar area, turning and jiggling the patient until all fluid filled spaces of the brain are filled with air—a crude method of examining the brain.

After the year in radiology I was second registrar in internal medicine for a year during which time I was in the late stages of pregnancy with our third child, Christine. There I was one day—8-months pregnant—resuscitating a man, my big belly hampering my efforts. This was 1967, a time when visibly pregnant American women teachers were not allowed in the classroom. Danes had no such concerns about offending young children's sensibilities, and though one could argue that my physical condition interfered with my job, that was hardly the case: the man survived.

By being a second registrar in internal medicine I was not aiming to become an internist; a year of internal medicine was necessary for any doctor who planned to become a specialist of any kind in Denmark. On the internal medicine floor there were a lot of routine cases, people one would not think of hospitalizing today—patients with hypertension, patients who needed their insulin doses adjusted, never mind that the hospital was not the best place to do that.

The patients that I remember best were a group of older women, hospitalized together in one ward, a kind of horror show of far advanced breast cancers, ulcerating, putrid cancers that had spread too far to be amenable to radical surgery or radiation therapy. These patients were there for palliative care long before we talked about palliative care as an option for end-stage disease, and on rounds there was talk of their soon being ready to go home, though everyone knew they were not going anywhere. It was painful for me to walk into that ward, not only because there was nothing I or anyone could offer in the way of a cure, but mostly because none of these women had been told her diagnosis. Physicians higher up than me may have told the family, but not the patients. There was a conspiracy of silence, which weighed heavily on everyone, as the family didn't want to burden the patient and make her lose hope. Doctors didn't want to talk to the patients about their diagnoses; how could you tell patients that their disease was hopeless? Not that the patients didn't know, they did, and they may have talked with each other about it, because from these women emanated an amazing sense of peace which they transmitted to their families—from whom they wanted to keep this terrible secret—and to the doctors. It was as if they sensed my unease when I walked into the room and they did their best to make me comfortable—me, the doctor, who should be healing them. So I just offered them relief from their physical pain and talked to them about their lives and families. This deceit, so hurtful to everyone involved, was practiced for years in Europe and around the globe making it very difficult to deal with cancer patients, and it resulted in most physicians keeping their distance from these patients. Fortunately we are now much more honest with patients and families.

Other experiences were more uplifting and less horrifying. One morning it was my turn to inspect the corpse in the morgue that had been brought in the day before. Danish law required that bodies be kept at the hospital morgue for 24 hours, at which time it was the duty of an internal medicine registrar to check on the corpse before it was released to the family. This was a simple task, one merely had to record: no pulse, no heartbeat, rigor mortis present or the like. Walking into the basement of one of the old buildings, I found the place deserted. Exposed piping rumbled and whistled as I made my way through long hallways to find the body lying on a stretcher in the unheated room that functioned as a morgue. I lifted the sheet to find the corpse of a man in his fifties. Rigor mortis had not set in; the body was pale. I placed my stethoscope on his chest, a routine gesture. He was dead, and I of course would hear nothing. Pulling the stethoscope away I absently grabbed his cold wrist checking for a pulse I wouldn't find. And then I stopped. Hadn't I heard something in his chest? Or was it just the pipes in the background? I put the stethoscope back on his chest and listened long and carefully and, sure enough, I heard a very faint and slow heartbeat. Obviously the man wasn't dead. I looked for a phone, but there was none and I had to run to a clinical area to call for help. Meanwhile I worried about the man, hoping no one would take him away while I was gone. I called the floor asking for a porter to bring the man to internal medicine.

While waiting for the porter, I read the information in the man's chart. He had been brought in *DOA* twenty-four hours before. Having spent the evening at the bars, he had fallen into a drunken sleep behind the wheel, just as he was about to start his car to go home at midnight. It was a very cold night. He was found the next morning, frozen stiff with no heartbeat and brought to the morgue. After the porter brought the man upstairs to the internal medicine department, we put him into a hospital bed and warmed him up. He walked out of the hospital a week later.

In Viborg, Hans and I contemplated how we would continue our medical studies when Hans finished his military duty. We could stay in Denmark, and slowly over a period of about eight to fourteen years prepare ourselves for board certification in a specialty, or go back to the United States for a residency that would take two or three years. We had liked the way medicine was practiced and taught in the United States, so we began looking at programs there in our chosen fields. Encouraged by Dr. Hellerstein at Children's Mercy Hospital in Kansas City, MO and with his recommendation, I had chosen pediatrics. Hans's interest lay in internal medicine, and as he would soon find out, specifically in gastroenterology. Several programs on the East Coast were attractive, but we didn't like the thought of living in a big American city for three years with our young children. We therefore applied to the Mayo Clinic in Minnesota. This for me had the added benefit that pediatric residents were on-call only every third day and night and not every other day and night, as was the case in Boston-area institutions.

With three children, even being on-call every third night would be hard, but we had enlisted a mature Danish woman, Mette, to come with us to be our nanny and housekeeper. That we found her, and that she consented to accompany us and eventually stayed for three years, was an absolute miracle: what we were about to undertake would never have worked without her.

3. United States 1970

Medicine is learned by the bedside and not in the classroom...See,
and then reason and compare and control. But see first.

Sir William Osler 1849-1919

A nurse paged me and I called her right back. "I want you immediately for the fifteen-year-old girl with gastroenteritis," she said. "I just went to do her vital signs and she's breathing rapidly, she is blue, and I'm now giving her oxygen. I've also called Bob [the chief resident]."

Arriving in the room a few minutes later, Bob and I found the patient not breathing. I quickly began mouth-to-mouth resuscitation. We were in Rochester, Minnesota, on the pediatric floor of St. Mary's Hospital. The fifteen-year-old had not been thought to be critical and there was no emergency cart in the room. She had arrived that morning with persistent vomiting, fever, and a presumptive diagnosis of viral gastroenteritis. Throughout the day she had become somewhat confused and had rapidly progressed to tachypnea and now respiratory arrest. This was the first time I had given mouth-to-mouth respiration. Doing this was a reflexive action that I would not contemplate doing a few years later. Fortunately, within seconds the nurse was there with a bag and mask and we began ventilating the patient.

The rapid progression of the patient's symptoms put in doubt the original presumptive diagnosis. What was going on here? Bob and I stayed up the entire night caring for this previously healthy young girl in the pediatric intensive care unit, yet, despite our efforts, by morning she was dead. At that time we did not know what we were dealing with and this death affected us deeply. But this is what I love about medicine—not the death but the detective work that goes into making a diagnosis: the search for clues. What we knew was that the girl had a fever for which she had been treated at home with aspirin, her blood ammonia was high, and she had cerebral edema, which we had treated without success and without changing the course of her illness. The detective work put us on a path and the autopsy confirmed our suspicions.

This was the first case of Reye's syndrome seen at the Mayo Clinic. In 1963, Dr. Douglas Reye had described the condition for the first time and over the years it became apparent that it occurred exclusively in children. A link between the syndrome, high fever, and aspirin was also documented. During research on patients who died from Reye's syndrome over the next ten years, this link became even stronger. In the 1980s, the Center for Disease Control cautioned against giving aspirin to children with fevers and the incidence of the disease dropped from about five hundred cases per year in the U.S. population to just two to three.

Hans and I had arrived in Rochester in 1969 for our residencies. Here we were somewhat isolated and the staff did not reach out to us socially to the degree they had in Kansas City. The Mayo Clinic at that time had five hundred residents and eight hundred consultants, making any encounter less personal. All residents worked hard, and while the married residents' wives formed a mutually supportive community, I, as a working female physician, was not part of it. We socialized little. When not working our priority was our children.

We were four female pediatric residents in our program of whom only one was American; the other two were Japanese. I failed to notice significant discrimination on a daily basis, but I had the sense that female residents were considered less capable than male. This was evidenced in at least one obvious way. For a time during the second year, one of the second-year residents was chief resident, the person who oversaw the other residents on the hospital service. When I became aware that female residents were not considered for this, I questioned a female consultant who had recently graduated from the program. Her comment, "Well, that's just the way it is," revealed an acquiescence that wasn't helpful. I talked to the section chief. I don't remember the discussion, but the result was that I became the first female chief resident in the pediatric program. I received snide remarks from male consultants that I ran the service with an iron hand. Maybe this was just their way of saying that they approved of the job I was doing, but it could also be the common story of competent women being perceived as aggressive.

Around this same time, I received an invitation to join the Phi Beta Kappa Honor Society. I had no clue what this was. I asked the same woman consultant and she told me it was an honor. "Yes, and so what," I thought. She didn't really convey to me that this was an honor I should accept, so I didn't. Besides, I still saw myself as the outsider. This was not something that would be understood in the Danish context. As I write this, I have just finished reading Justice Sonia Sotomayor's memoirs, and I realize that I have at least one thing in common with this eminent Puerto Rican immigrant. While at Princeton, she too had no idea what the Phi Beta Kappa Honor Society was, but someone convinced her to accept the invitation to join. I have also recently read Sheryl Sandberg's memoir *Lean In: Women, Work and the Will to Lead* (2013) and have been amazed to read that many American women feel fraudulent when they are praised for their accomplishments. I had no problems accepting praise especially when I thought it was due, and unlike Sheryl Sandberg, I never believed that my failures were due to an inherent lack of ability. I consider myself lucky to have had that attitude; it became helpful to me in my career. I believed then as I do now that this had much to do with the way I was raised, with attitudes toward women in Denmark, and that women in the U.S. received—and maybe still receive—different cues from society.

I loved the hospital service more than any other service, but spent only two quarters there during my two years. Some time was spent in the pediatric outpatient department at the Mayo Clinic, where we rotated taking calls. This was a time when home visits were still made, and the clinic put a car at the on-call person's disposal. For me, home visits were dissatisfying, but for families, valuable. I disliked the visits since I could only make presumptive diagnoses. I could either reassure the family that the child would recover with symptomatic treatment—though I might prescribe antibiotics if there was an obvious ear-infection—or, if the patient was very sick and I didn't know what was going on, encourage them to come to the hospital emergency room to see me for further evaluation and tests. To the parents, however, this holding of hands was important, and despite my misgivings I acknowledged this: to have to take a feverish, sick child out at night—especially if it is to a cold car in the midst of winter—and to sit for hours in an emergency room waiting to be seen, is a hardship. For a single parent with more than one child it poses added difficulties.

Once, however, in one of those blizzards that blow in from the prairie and create wind tunnels between the Mayo buildings, I got a call to see a patient at the outskirts of town. I told the mother that I thought it best if she could bring the child to the emergency room for me to see; the family apparently had a truck. The car the clinic had placed at my disposal was a small passenger car, and of course in those days there was no front-wheel drive, so I knew I had a very good chance of getting stuck. I thought this arrangement was agreed to when five minutes later I got a call from one of the consultants. The mother, who obviously knew him, had called him to complain, and he was now overriding my decision. I explained my reasons, but no, he wanted me to drive to the house and see the child. I had always liked Dr. Logan. He was an older consultant in pediatric allergy and a very kind man. But that night I was not particularly happy with him, and I swore under my breath as I made my way across town to the patient. It took much longer than it should have, because there were streets steep enough that the car could not make it and I had to take detours, but I didn't get stuck. I examined the patient, who was not very sick and could easily have waited until morning.

While some of Dr. Logan's generation may have deplored the demise of the family physician who made home visits, it clearly is not an efficient use of a physician's time.

As pediatric residents we also rotated through pediatric subspecialty services such as endocrinology, neurology, or cardiology. Liking the clear-cut hemodynamics of the heart, and enjoying the puzzle of determining which congenital malformation was causing a particular change in those dynamics, I was especially enamored of cardiology. At that time, arriving at a diagnosis began with listening to the heart, identifying the differing quality of murmurs, and making a presumptive diagnosis based on history, symptoms, auscultation, and other physical findings. Then the diagnosis was confirmed or ruled out with catheterization and contrast-enhanced echocardiography, as well as the measuring of oxygen-saturations and pressures. More sophisticated procedures were yet to come, and no scans were available at the time.

When after two years I sat for my pediatric boards in New Orleans, one of the younger consultants, Dr. Cloutier, an endocrinologist in the pediatric department at the Mayo Clinic, was an examiner. This man was my most ardent supporter—sadly he committed suicide some years later. On returning to Rochester after the exam, he let the department know that I had outperformed my male fellow residents and this was taken as surprising news by everyone but me. Most of my exams in medical school in Denmark had been oral exams, and I thrived when being tested in that format, especially when I felt secure in my knowledge, as I did at the exam in New Orleans. Multiple-choice questions were quite another issue, something I had had very little exposure to, and those were not part of the boards at the time.

My program was only two years long, whereas Hans's was a three-year program, so when I was asked to stay on for a third year I spent about six months in pediatric cardiology. To my surprise, there was now no limit to what I could do, and I often felt challenged making rounds alone on post-operative cardiac patients, somewhat overwhelmed by the trust placed in me. I also had the joy of being the chief resident in pediatrics again.

Hans and I both immensely enjoyed being residents at the Mayo Clinic and greatly appreciated what we learned there. Two things stood out: we developed good bedside manners—something that had not been emphasized in Denmark—and we became better clinicians, learning to take a thorough history by listening to what the patient told us, and to do a proper clinical evaluation by listening to what the patient's body told us.

At the end of our program we again returned to Denmark. Assured that we were well qualified, we looked forward to working and sharing our knowledge as first registrars in the pediatric and internal medicine departments, respectively, at Aalborg Sygehus Nord in Aalborg. Our chiefs appreciated us because we had a solid base of knowledge, and if stumped by a problem we knew how to find answers, something not drilled into our co-workers.

The chief of the pediatric department, *overlæge* Hansted, had an interest in neonatal care, and a number of newborns with problems were hospitalized in a special room in the pediatric ward; there was no newborn intensive care unit at the hospital. *Overlæge* Hansted had one idiosyncrasy. It was now known that using respirators to treat babies with respiratory distress could lead to chronic lung disease. Because of this he was violently against the use of any respirators in newborns. Instead he had the nurses ventilate the babies manually with bag and mask. This worked reasonably well in mild respiratory distress, but it presupposed good staffing because one person would be tied up with one baby for the entire shift, even though the nurses relieved each other in the task. Working with these newborns sparked my interest in neonatology and I had many discussions with my chief about the treatment of respiratory distress. I wanted him to be more accepting of the use of respirators so we might save more babies, but he was adamant: no respirators for his babies.

In Denmark there was—and still is—a specific hierarchy among hospital physicians. At the top is the *overlæge,* the chief of the department. Then there is one or several first registrars depending on the size of the service, and below them are four or five second registrars. The chief of the department often has his own agenda, however, and is not always sensitive to the younger people in his department. Hans and I, who were of a more egalitarian bent, were bothered by this prima donna behavior.

Daily, after rounds in the pediatric department, all physicians met to discuss cases encountered on the wards. The meeting did not start until *overlæge* Hansted was present. He was a kind and knowledgeable man whom I enjoyed, but he was always late. Day after day he failed to show up at the agreed-upon time. One day after waiting for over half an hour I, as the second-in-command, decided to start the meeting. A half hour later *overlæge* Christian Hansted burst through the door, his arms filled with papers. I rose to let him have his seat. We were in the midst of discussing a patient, and when he realized this, he looked confused, seemingly failing to understand what was going on, "So...you have started?"

"Yes, I thought we should start instead of just sitting here waiting. Some of us are not done with our rounds, and we would like to go back to finish our work."

Christian Hansted, the perfect gentleman of the old school, started explaining what had happened on this particular day, "I apologize, but something came up...a bureaucrat from city hall needed to talk with me, there was much to discuss...financing...and I lost track of time." As he spoke, he became defensive, and a tad indignant. "I really have no control over the city bureaucracy."

I was unsympathetic. "You set the time," I said. "If you can't be here, surely you can have no objection that we start without you."

As I write this, I almost become embarrassed at my former self's assertiveness. Being *overlæge* was a big deal then. You were the king of your department, and your underlings fell in line, doing what you told them to do. *Overlæge* Christian Hansted was also puzzled: he genuinely didn't understand why I should be upset, and I suspect he thought that, incredibly, I lacked good manners. This kind of insubordination was not appreciated, and would probably eventually have counted against me had I sought a promotion. As things turned out I need not have worried.

Hans and I hoped one day to become chiefs of departments at a provincial hospital. Few specialists were in private practice in Denmark. Therefore all specialists vied for the few positions at the top of the pyramid at hospitals around the country. We, however, worried that we might not be able to get positions in the same city. Furthermore, it also soon became clear, that there was only one way to the top: the Danish way. That we had chosen to get our education in the U.S. without being sent by a department in the Danish health system, was a faux pas that was near unforgivable. Before leaving the United States we had both passed our specialty boards, but that held no water with the Danish health system. It provided no shortcut; we had to start over in an orderly fashion, climbing the ladder with the rest. This also included showing the appropriate respect for our superiors. There is also a peculiar attitude toward those who don't follow the beaten path, an attitude recognized in all of Scandinavia. The Danes call it the *Jantelaw* and it has ten rules, among them: you're not to think you are anything special, you're not to think *you* are smarter than *us*, you're not to think *you* know more than *us*, you're not to think *you* can teach *us* anything, and so on. Hans and I were met with some of that attitude.

After just three months we realized that this was not an environment in which we could thrive. We began thinking about returning to the United States and started looking for jobs in the Midwest. We would no longer be able to enter the U.S. on student visas; we needed to immigrate. Fortunately, that was not difficult at the time, as the quota for immigrants from Denmark was never filled and U.S.-trained foreign physicians were welcomed by the United States.

Our decision to immigrate dismayed Hans's father who with our return from Rochester had looked forward to having his oldest son nearby. His mother was more accepting. My parents who had spent much of their life away from family said nothing. I am sure they were saddened, but they seemed to understand our decision. Both sets of parents already had one child in North America: Hans's sister, Karen and family had settled in Newfoundland, Canada after her husband finished his training in Kansas City. My younger sister, Anna, had moved from Ireland to Minneapolis five years before. Each set of parents was left with three children in Denmark, a small consolation: the prodigal son or daughter, the one who had sought his own path, is the one longed for. Today I have my children and grandchildren nearby, and I acutely feel our parents' pain. It would be difficult for me to have a child and his family in Europe, but I am also equally certain that Hans and I would not have been happy in Denmark. Our professional lives would have lacked the challenges we have thrived on since making this difficult decision. We had regrets that our children would grow up without having a close relationship with their grandparents and cousins. But there were positives: our situation did not compare to that of the immigrants of old. We could fly back to Denmark to visit from time to time.

The next summer Hans and I took a two-week vacation. We told no one at Aalborg Hospital where we were going, left the kids with my parents, traveled to the United States for job interviews, and sat for the Minnesota State Medical Boards in Minneapolis. We had two job interviews lined up, but after visiting the Duluth Clinic and seeing the city of Duluth we decided it had all we wished for: jobs for both of us, a good medical community, a university and medical school, a large body of water on which to sail—important for those coming from the island country of Denmark—and a beautiful setting with easy access to the outdoors. We therefore canceled our other job interview, putting all of our eggs in one basket.

Upon returning to Denmark, we awaited the results of the Minnesota State Board Exams. Once they were available in mid-August, the Duluth Clinic asked Hans to start his job on September 1. I planned to get the kids settled in Duluth before starting my job in November. Out of necessity we gave only two weeks notice at our jobs in Denmark. This caused a minor uproar, another faux pas. Four weeks notice was the rule. With that and after emptying our meager pension accounts, we had effectively burned our bridges in our home country.

II. Pioneering Newborn Intensive Care

4. Duluth, Minnesota 1973

Whether born from experience or inherent physiological or cultural differences, our gender and national origins may and will make a difference...

Sonia Sotomayor

We arrived in Duluth just before Labor Day in 1973. This was our fifth move within seven years. All my siblings, except for my schizophrenic brother, were wanderers, hungering for new places and new experiences, not content to stay in one place for long. This was true for me as well. It appeared to us that this was also common in our new country: frequent moves were part of life for many Americans, be it in search of new educational venues or jobs. I was concerned that our children would be far from their nearest kin, but I rarely worried about the effect of our moves on them. Kids are resilient, especially if they are loved and in a stable family.

This last move therefore saw us in a situation we had not experienced before. We were now in a place where we would likely remain for the rest of our careers, maybe even our lives. Had we remained in Denmark and had we been forced to battle our way to the top of the pyramid, we would have had to move frequently, though within the country. So it was a relief in a way that we could finally think about putting down roots.

Partly due to the expense of moving, and partly because our house in Denmark had not sold, we arrived with only five hundred dollars to our names. However, since we both had signed on as physicians at the Duluth Clinic, a bank was easily persuaded to lend us enough to buy two cars and—besides the mortgage—the down payment for a house. Those were the days! Needing a place to live before the school year started, we bought a basic rambler that was sitting empty in the Lakeside neighborhood of Duluth, thinking we could always find a nicer house later. As it turned out, once we were settled and had started working, we had little time to think about another house, and "later" didn't happen until the kids had left home.

Mike and Peter enrolled at Ordean Junior High and Lakeside Elementary, respectively. In order to get the kids settled and our house organized, I had elected not to start my job right away; this was the first time I had taken a break in my career. With two months off, I achieved the first goal of getting the kids settled, but not the second of getting the house organized. Before leaving Denmark, Hans had made crates for our furniture and other possessions, which were loaded onto a freighter that would carry them across the ocean. However, instead of arriving in three weeks as promised, our possessions arrived three months later.

During those first two months I felt a little lost. We knew no one in town. The house contained only the beds we bought, the garden furniture that neighbors lent us, and camping kitchen gear, so I had plenty of time for four-year-old Christine. But as I wanted to ease her into attending the Montessori Nursery School, even she was not home all the time.

During this period, the enormity of the fact that we would be spending the rest of our lives in the U.S. hit me. Much of my life I had been a stranger in a foreign land and had enjoyed it in the certain conviction that eventually I would return *home*. In the hustle and bustle of moving and in the excited anticipation of our new life, the reality of our decision to emigrate had evaded me. Now I knew that not only would I live in the U.S. for the rest of my life, I would also likely die here. The latter bothered me. A Danish friend who had lived in the United States for twelve years had recently returned to Denmark because he couldn't bear the thought of dying so far from home. There was a reality to that, because for us Denmark was still *home*.

Transitions had always been difficult for me and this was no exception. Our roots—such as they were—had been torn up not once, but time and again. A tree can take just so many transplantations, but humans, I suppose, are more resilient, and though it would take time for us to feel at home in Duluth, we would eventually put down our roots here.

The first year was challenging for Michael, an 8th grader in junior high. Peter, in 4th grade, settled in more easily. Neither of them had language problems. Christine, however, had forgotten the English she had acquired in Rochester. In order to ease her into school, I initially took her to the Montessori school for only a couple of hours a week. She gradually reacquired enough English to communicate with her peers, adjusted to her new environment, and thrived.

That we never felt really lonesome during this time was due in large part to the very fortuitous presence of another Danish family in our immediate neighborhood with whom we soon established strong ties. Sven Hubner, a shipping agent, his wife Kitte, and their daughters Annelise and Karen, lived only a block away and eventually moved in just across the street from us. They became family to us. Over the years, we spent many happy times together.

Adjusting to my new job at the Duluth Clinic was also far from easy. Though I accept my share of the blame for not fitting into the pediatric department—as an introvert I most likely did not go out of my way to be congenial—the cause of my unhappiness lay in part with two of the older pediatricians, one of whom was vociferous in his contempt for me.

I was the first full-time woman physician to be employed at the Duluth Clinic. Another Danish woman, an internist, had practiced here for a number of years in a part-time capacity. There was only one other practicing woman physician in town, a surgeon, who was in practice with her surgeon brother. I was thus the first woman pediatrician and the second fulltime woman physician in the city's medical community.

For some of my older colleagues it was as if I was from another planet. Not only was I a foreigner, I had also taken a very different path in life, not just because I had gone to medical school in Denmark, but most significantly because I was female. When I first started my job, I thought I would belong; I had after all done my post-graduate training in the U.S. I had felt well accepted at Mayo, where of course there were many foreign graduates, a number of them women. But that was not to be here. For my new colleagues a woman in the workplace meant a nurse or a secretary. I fell outside this category and the hierarchy among physicians was vague. Though one of my colleagues was the department head, a position occupied by department members on a rotating basis, I did not consider that I had a boss; I was in a partnership. If I reported to anyone, it was to the administration of the clinic.

As I sat in my office between patients, dictating, with my door open, I heard my older colleague making a fool of himself raging about my unworthiness. He was given to flowery language and epithets. Some years later I would have called him on it, but I knew I had no voice then. Had I said anything I would most likely have been asked to leave my position. The best I could do was to close my door so as not to have to listen to him. This kind of indirect attack is very destructive, and this one was meant to undermine me. Unfortunately I had no female colleagues to ask for advice, but because I felt very secure in my professional competence I refused to let it get me down.

After a year, new physicians were invited to become shareholders at the Clinic. No such offer was extended to me, though it was extended to Hans. My older colleague was behind this, I was sure, though a year later he must have caved in because then I became a shareholder. As I see it, the issue likely was that I didn't know how to sweet-talk "the guys;" I wanted to relate to them on a professional basis and when I received inappropriate comments and questions from them, such as, "I always knew you were a sweater girl" (lewd, sexist) and "Are you planning to have more children?" (inappropriate and illegal), I declined responding or commenting. From others, especially older non-pediatrician colleagues I heard, "Meet our attractive new physician..." While realizing it as a probable compliment I could not help but counter—in a bantering way—with "Would you say the same of a male physician?" I thought this ludicrous male condescension specifically American, and a mindset most Americans failed to recognize as inappropriate.

Fortunately, other older and younger members of the pediatric department were very supportive, and as it happened, I would eventually find my niche outside general pediatrics.

My unhappiness during that first year also derived from the fact that I was temperamentally best suited for dealing with acutely ill patients; office pediatrics did not excite me. For a time, I considered returning to the Mayo Clinic for training in pediatric cardiology—that wanderlust must have hit again—but Hans was quite happy in his work, so it was clear that was not an option.

Viewing my situation from today's perspective, one would think that mothers would have flocked to me—the first woman pediatrician in town—but that was far from the case. I think many women at the time wanted to have a male physician, a paternal figure who would dictate to them how to bring up their children, à la Dr. Spock. Since that time, I have talked to some of my previous patients' mothers, who said they loved having me as a pediatrician because I was a real person, someone who dealt with them on an equal footing, someone who was not only a physician but also a mother, but I am sure that this was not what most women were looking for then. When I was on call I felt that many women had been conditioned by their pediatrician to rely on him in most matters regarding their children's health and safety. They did not seem willing to make decisions about their offspring's health on their own, even in trivial matters. Young mothers of today are much better informed and make more independent decisions.

After a weekend on call where I received a hundred phone calls, many of them concerning questions that the mother easily could have answered herself, I was more than ready to give up being a pediatrician and focus on neonatology, a new and exciting field toward which I was drawn.

5. First Transport

It is not easy to be a pioneer—but oh, it is fascinating! I would not trade one moment, even the worst moment, for all the riches in the world.

Elizabeth Blackwell M.D., first U.S. woman physician (1821-1910)

It was the winter of 1974. I had started my pediatric practice at the Duluth Clinic in November of 1973, but was spending increasing amounts of time at the hospital taking care of sick newborns. At St. Mary's Hospital, the hospital associated with and connected by a skywalk to the Duluth Clinic, I had one of the nurseries with three or four isolettes and a radiantly heated open bed at my disposal, but my resources were few, as the neonatal intensive care unit was yet to be built. We had no wall suction or oxygen, relying instead on portable suction and oxygen tanks.

On this particular day I received a call from the nuns at the now defunct St. Joseph's Hospital in Superior, Wisconsin, just across St. Louis Bay from Duluth. They had twin premature babies who were not doing well and wondered if they could be transferred to my care. This was the first call for transfer I had received, and were we to transfer the babies it would be one of our first transports. I was young and enthusiastic about providing neonatal intensive care. So, being new to Duluth winters and failing to realize the toll the weather might take on these premature twins, I quickly agreed to go get them. I consulted with our respiratory therapist, Candy, and her husband, Harvey, who owned Gold Cross Ambulance. We had no transport incubator. Instead we took the top half of a heated isolette and secured it to a stretcher. Having no electrical outlets in the ambulance for the isolette, we covered it in heated blankets so that it would retain its warmth. Thus prepared, we arrived at St. Joseph's Hospital.

We entered, leaving behind the frigid air. Our boots echoed in the empty hallway as the stretcher clunked across the floor. Hastening toward us with tiny fleeting steps was a Sister in white flowing robes who was anxious to direct us to our patients.

"Thank you for coming," she said, as if we had graciously consented to be her dinner guests. The brown and white linoleum floor of the hallway had an oft-scrubbed, worn-down look; walls of a vapid beige reached the tiled, dropped ceilings; light from underpowered bulbs in round milky glass fixtures provided shadowy lighting. Leading us down the hallway past varnished, wooden doors on either side, she arrived at the elevator, pressed a button, and said, "I don't think those babies are going to make it."

The doors pulled away and we entered the large elevator. Snow melted in puddles around our boots. I shed my gloves and unbuttoned my winter coat in anticipation of entering a hot nursery. While we ascended two floors, Sister told us about the babies.

"They're a week old. We've tried to keep them warm and have fed them small amounts of milk. They seemed to be doing well for a few days…then became jaundiced…we had them under phototherapy…now they are throwing up, their bellies are distended, and we can't feed them. They hardly move anymore. They need IV fluids…and we can't provide that."

The door of the elevator opened and Sister now led us to the nursery, which had yellowish-brown tiles and a large glass pane toward the hallway. While taking off my coat, I felt a draft of cool air from the outside windows. The babies were in a heated isolette of a type that had single walls and a red flag at the back that could be raised if more than 40 percent oxygen was needed. We plugged in our isolette, which by now was no longer warm, and began heating it to its maximum temperature. I opened the portholes of the babies' isolette to examine them. They were both dressed and wrapped in blankets.

"We had trouble keeping them warm, so we bundled them up next to each other," Sister said.

"They're getting oxygen?" I asked, as I noticed the tubing connecting the isolette to a large oxygen tank.

"Yes," Sister said. "They were looking a little blue, so we turned on the oxygen. But they've received no more than 40 percent." Oh, yes, I thought, the infamous forty per cent, this magic number that one should not exceed if one wanted to minimize the risk of blindness in premature infants. The problem was that these babies still had blue lips and nail beds, and they needed more oxygen. To Sister's consternation I flipped the flag up. I diplomatically told her there was no magic upper limit of 40 percent when providing oxygen to prematures. This 40 percent concept had arisen from past history. During the forties and fifties, increased survival was noted in prematures who received liberal amounts of oxygen. This was good news, but subsequently it was found that prematures who had received more than 40 percent oxygen had been much more prone to developing retinopathy of prematurity (which leads to varying degrees of blindness) than babies who had received less. Thus arose the myth of the 40 percent, and isolettes were subsequently developed that could deliver no more than 40 percent, unless a specific red-flagged action was taken. By 1974 it had long been realized that babies need as much oxygen as it takes to render them "pink." We now titrated oxygen given to babies against the oxygen saturation of their blood. But the old concept of "no more than 40 percent" was slow to die.

In view of the less-than-ideal temperature in the room, I had closed the portholes and decided to postpone further examination of the babies, until they were in the nursery at St. Mary's Hospital. When our isolette was heated again, we put both babies inside it, surrounding them with gloves filled with hot water wrapped in receiving blankets so as not to burn the babies. Candy and I beat a hasty retreat, since we had no way of giving them oxygen until we got them to the ambulance.

Today I would have been unwilling to undertake a transport with the equipment I had then, but if I hadn't taken them, the babies would surely have died at the referring hospital. It was worth a chance, it seemed, and furthermore, we learned much from this. Over time, these types of transports were refined. Special transport incubators came on the market with a battery that kept them heated during transport. They also had a small oxygen tank, so that oxygen could be administered during transport from nursery to ambulance. As we gained knowledge about the ideal thermal environment for neonates, babies arrived at our Neonatal Intensive Care Unit (NICU) with normal temperatures and in more stable conditions, which greatly enhanced their chances of survival.

As soon as the stretcher was clamped down, we connected the isolette to oxygen at ten liters per minute, covered it in blankets, and headed for Duluth via the Blatnik Bridge—a distance of less than ten miles. From time to time we lifted the blankets to be sure that the babies were okay, but the lighting was so poor that we could barely discern their skin color.

With outside temperatures well below zero and a stiff northeast wind off Lake Superior, the chill factor was close to forty below. Snow was piled high along the streets. The large spacious ambulance could not stay warm in the cold weather. I was happy to have on my heavy winter coat.

The trip took no more than fifteen minutes, yet when we were back in St. Mary's nursery, the isolette was no longer warm. Quickly we transferred the babies into warm isolettes. Admission temperatures were 96.5° F., not a good sign. In reviewing the records from St. Joseph's I saw that their temperatures had been running between 97° and 97.5°F. These prolonged low temperatures may well have set off a domino effect of increased oxygen needs with resultant metabolic and respiratory acidosis leading to poor perfusion of the gut and secondary feeding intolerance. Whatever had happened, I realized the babies did not have much of a chance. I tried hard to stabilize their temperatures, correct their acidosis, and provide appropriate fluids and electrolytes, but things continued to go downhill. Urine output decreased, their abdomens became increasingly distended, and finally they expired several hours after admission. The parents, who had not been present at St. Joseph's Hospital, came shortly after the babies had been admitted to St. Mary's Hospital and spent their last few hours with them.

These babies' course is not surprising, considering all we have learned as the specialty of neonatology has evolved. Looking back, one realizes that had these babies been born at one of the university centers that were the Meccas of neonatal knowledge at the time, they might well have lived. In the seventies, the managing of preemies in an intensive care setting took place mainly at academic centers. Regional NICUs and neonatal transports were just in the process of being developed.

It should also be noted that before NICUs came into existence, in the U.S. and elsewhere in the developed world, one took no active stance with prematures. One provided supportive care, warmth, feedings, and oxygen. If that failed to carry the babies through, one accepted that they were doomed to die.

Neonatal transport, interestingly enough, began as early as 1900 when Dr. Joseph DeLee of the Chicago Lying-In Hospital developed the first mobile incubator for premature babies. This so-called "hand ambulance" provided warmth while transporting premature infants to the hospital following home births. In 1914, the first dedicated neonatal transport vehicle in the United States was donated to the Chicago Department of Health by Dr. Martin Couney—*The Incubator Doctor*—(see later) following the closure of the Chicago World's Fair, where the vehicle had been used to transport premature babies to the neonatal exhibit. The first organized transport program in the United States was not in place, however, until 1948 when the New York Department of Health, in conjunction with area hospitals, developed the New York Premature Infant Transport Service.

In regional communities like ours, neonatal transport was just about to begin. Our first transport was not a success, and I do not remember undertaking another transport of preemies until our neonatal unit was built and a more organized transport system had been developed.

6. First Ventilator Patient

Billy was born in 1974. His mother's pregnancy with him was unremarkable except that he was overdue. This was the mother's third pregnancy and she was not overly concerned when her bag of waters broke at home. She called her husband and waited patiently for him to return to their home in northern Wisconsin; only then was she ready for the twenty-five-mile trip to the hospital in Duluth. Labor progressed normally. There was green meconium in her fluid, but as there had been much amniotic fluid, little attention was paid to that. Besides, meconium is common in post-term babies and, anyway, the baby was in no distress: the fetal heart tones were normal. Delivery was by the vaginal route, and at birth the nurse suctioned Billy's mouth for moderate amounts of meconium-stained fluid. His Apgar scores were good and so were his vital signs. He was taken to the nursery.

Within hours he began having respiratory distress and became blue. His color improved with oxygen, but the respiratory distress continued and in fact worsened as the hours passed. I was the new kid on the block, a young pediatrician with an interest in neonatal medicine, and by now care of sick newborns had shifted to me. I was called to see Billy. The NICU was still in the planning stage and as yet no infant at St. Mary's Hospital had been treated on a ventilator. The nursery was divided into two rooms: a small pink nursery and a larger nursery, with a cleaning room in between. The larger room and the cleaning area would become the new NICU. Meanwhile, the large nursery had become my temporary unit where I cared for sick newborns. We moved Billy there. Transferring him to the closest NICU at the University of Minnesota in Minneapolis was not considered, as transport of neonates had not yet been developed.

An Ohio bed (a square open bed with radiant heat above it) sat proudly in the corner of my "neonatal unit." Billy, a big baby, took up much of the three-by-three foot bed. His head was placed in a transparent acrylic oxygen hood to better deliver high concentrations of oxygen and humidity. We periodically drew blood from him to assess his respiratory status. As the CO_2 (carbon-dioxide) levels in his blood began to rise, it became evident that Billy was getting worse. Respiratory therapy was a new field at St. Mary's Hospital, and the head of the department was Candy, who had trained in Rochester in adult respiratory therapy. By evening, Billy's CO_2s had climbed to levels where he would soon need a respirator if he were to survive. There were adult respirators at St. Mary's, but no infant respirators. How were we to ventilate him? Certainly not manually, if I could help it. Our quandary was solved when Candy called Rochester and asked if they could send an infant respirator to Duluth. They could, and overnight the State Patrol brought it to us. It was an adult respirator that had been retrofitted with smaller tubing more appropriate for infants.

Now we needed to have Billy intubated. I don't remember if I had learned to intubate then, or if I learned that later. I remember teaching sessions we arranged at one point in time for residents and nurses at the medical school at the University of Minnesota, Duluth. Cats under ketamine-induced anesthesia were our test animals. Cats are excellent models for intubating human newborns as their tracheas are about the size of newborn's tracheas. Cats, however, have teeth—sharp teeth—where infants have none, so it was difficult to manipulate the laryngoscope past the teeth. The ketamine also meant that though the cats were immobile and couldn't move, bite, or scratch, their cough reflexes remained intact, and as one entered the endotracheal tube into their tracheas, a hot stream of cat breath was blasted into one's face as the cat violently tried to cough up the tube. It is far easier to intubate babies.

Candy and I had carefully studied how to ventilate Billy: what volume of air to give him with every breath, what maximum inspiratory pressure, what end-expiratory pressure, and what respiratory rate was appropriate. We got the respirator ready to go, and then I intubated Billy— or maybe one of the anesthesiologists did it. This is usually not an easy task in a strong term newborn as he will fight the tube, but Billy must have been exhausted from hours of breathing hard and did not fight. We listened carefully as we hand ventilated him to make sure that the endotracheal tube had not been advanced too far into the right main-stem bronchus, then taped down the tube, connected it to the respirator, and called for a portable x-ray. Scrutinizing the x-ray, we found that the ET-tube was in the right position and the lungs were better expanded, but not over-expanded. It was trial by fire, and Billy was our unfortunate—or fortunate—guinea pig. Miracle of miracles: Billy settled down as he was ventilated. Subsequent blood gases also showed that the CO_2 level was dropping, and his respiratory acidosis was resolving.

We soon learned that without trained staff, it was scary to have a baby intubated. Secretions and mucus tend to accumulate in the tube and if not suctioned periodically, the tube may plug off. Candy instructed our nurses on how to suction, and she or I remained close to the nursery until we knew that Billy had stabilized. I treated him with antibiotics to prevent pneumonia. There was certainly a lot of undeserved luck involved. Though it seemed as if Billy was sick for a long time, he had none of the—sometimes devastating—complications of meconium aspiration: pneumothorax and pulmonary hypertension. As I remember it, he remained stable and within less than a week we were able to wean him off the respirator. He was not fed during that time, but he quickly took to breastfeeding after he was extubated, and the family was able to take a healthy child home at the end of ten days.

With time, a planned approach to handling the baby with meconium-stained fluid would be developed, whereby the obstetrician cleared the baby's mouth for meconium as soon as the head came out, and the neonatologist attending the birth aspirated the lungs for meconium after delivery. With that approach, respiratory distress from meconium and complications thereof were avoided, and we would eventually see few of those kinds of patients in our NICUs.

These were the inauspicious beginnings of neonatal care in Duluth, and soon more difficult patients would come my way.

7. The Incubator Doctor

Some twenty years ago, I was astounded to come across the following colorful chapter in the history of the care of premature babies, and I was amazed at the results it had produced. I discovered this long after St. Mary's NICU had been started, but it is a chapter that bears telling in the context of this memoir about neonates and neonatal care.

An obituary in the *New York Times* in 1950 read as follows:

> "Dr. Martin Couney, the *Incubator Doctor,* died last night in his home. He was a specialist in the care of prematurely born infants and had shown such infants to the public for an admission price at fairs and other exhibitions throughout the United States and in Europe for more than 50 years. He was 80 years old at the time of his death. Born in Germany he had studied at Breslau, Berlin, and Leipzig, receiving an M.D. and later in Paris under Dr. Pierre Budin, noted pediatrician who developed a method of saving the prematurely born."

In order to understand Dr. Couney's peculiar life endeavor, some background is necessary. In the nineteenth century—in Europe as well as in the United States—infant mortality rates were exceedingly high. During this period most infants, including premature babies, were born at home; only poor mothers delivered in hospitals. Doctors attended neither home nor hospital deliveries, and if one was called, it was to attend to the mother. Care of the baby was the mother's domain. Many premature and sick babies died within the first couple of days from hypothermia, infection, or dehydration.

In the 1870s, after huge losses sustained in the Franco-Prussian War, and with falling birth rates, France decided that the country could no longer afford these high mortality rates. Men were needed for the industry, the military, and the colonies. Dr. Stephane Tarnier, an obstetrician at the Port Royal Maternity Hospital in Paris, was inspired to develop an incubator for premature infants after seeing a chicken incubator at the Paris Zoo. Tarnier's baby incubator was heated with hot-water bottles that a nurse exchanged every three hours. Dr. Tarnier would subsequently claim that the use of his self-invented incubator for premature babies had cut the mortality rate of these infants from 66 to 38 percent.

Regardless of the dubious veracity of his claim, he got the attention of the Paris Municipal Board, which quickly set up maternity wards at most of its hospitals and outfitted them with incubators, midwives, and doctors with special training. These *services des débiles,* or "wards for weaklings," admitted and treated all premature and sick babies brought from home as well as those of the very poor who had delivered in the hospital. But alarmingly, they did not attain the success Dr. Tarnier had claimed; their mortality rate was 70 percent. The main reason for this was that babies often were in very poor condition by the time the mothers surrendered them to the hospital at two to three days of age.

In 1895, Dr. Pierre Budin followed Dr. Tarnier as chief obstetrician at Port Royal Maternity (he also billed himself as a pediatrician). He realized that to reduce the mortality rate of premature and "weak" infants, he needed the mothers' cooperation. He identified three problem areas in the care of these babies: temperature control, delivery and quality of feeding, and susceptibility to disease. For the most part the Tarnier incubator solved the temperature problem. For feedings, Dr. Budin insisted on breast milk from the mother or from wet-nurses. If the infant couldn't suck, Budin had the mother hand-express milk allowing it to trickle into the baby's mouth; he also encouraged the use of nasal, spoon, or gavage feedings. To combat disease, he instituted several ground rules: the necessity of separating the wet-nurses' own babies from the prematures, isolating sick prematures, sterilizing milk and bottles, and having mothers and wet-nurses wash and put on gowns before caring for the baby.

The mortality rate of these premature and sick babies dropped to 50 percent. The guidelines developed by Dr. Budin were essential to improving neonatal survival, and the entire Western world slowly adopted them with very little adjustment. At the time of Dr. Budin's death in 1907, he was hailed as having saved "a battalion of infants" for France.

In 1889 in Nice, France, Dr. Alexandre Lion had developed and patented an incubator that was far superior to Dr. Tarnier's. It was a large metal apparatus equipped with a thermostat and independent forced ventilation. It was rather expensive, but Dr. Lion was an entrepreneur as well as an inventor. He set up nurseries in storefronts on busy streets, so passers-by could stop in and pay a fee to watch—behind a glass wall—how a premature nursery worked.

Eventually, in 1896, Dr. Lion exhibited his incubator at the Berlin Exposition, where it became a huge sensation. His assistant, Dr. Couney—the *Incubator Doctor* of future fame—was sent by Professor Czerny, an illustrious Berlin obstetrician, to the Empress Augusta Viktoria to ask her permission to recruit prematures from her Charity Hospital (today the Charité is *the* university hospital in Berlin). The Empress readily agreed—premature babies had little chance of survival anyway. Dr. Couney brought six incubators and an entourage of Dr. Budin's nurses to the exhibition, calling the show *Das Kinderbrutanstalt*: the Child Hatchery. This baby show caught the imagination of the Berlin public to the degree that soon rousing songs about it were heard in beer halls and nightclubs. The exhibit was located in the amusement section of the Exposition—something that rankled Dr. Couney—between an ethnic village and The Tyrolean Yodelers. Several batches of infants were "hatched" and there were no deaths, according to Couney.

The next year, in 1897, Dr. Couney had his own exhibition at the Victorian Era Exhibition in Earl's Court in London. It was an overwhelming success, despite the fact that no premature babies could be procured in London. Dr. Couney, resourceful as ever, requested Dr. Budin's help and the latter shipped "three wicker baskets full of Parisian premature babies to London." (*Pediatrics* 1979). Considering the hazard inherent in transporting prematures, one tends to question the veracity of this story.

An editorial in the *Lancet* on February 5, 1898 noted that the introduction of incubators for babies into Britain had been well received, that the incubators were of highly reputable construction, and that the skilled attendants were trained not only in the care of babies and management of incubators, but were especially trained in the care of prematurely born and debilitated infants. Since the Victorian Era Exhibition as such was a serious exhibition of valuable arts and science, the editorial said, there was nothing derogatory in exhibiting the healing arts, especially as a healthy site had been chosen in the broadest part of the garden where there was plenty of fresh air. The editor did, however, warn the public of possible copycats who for profit might attempt to imitate the incubator show without knowing anything about incubators or the intricate care of prematures.

Later, at a Couney Exhibition at the 1901 Pan-American Exposition in Buffalo, New York, an observer noted the following (an extract of notes collected by Dr. William A. Silverman, published in an article "Incubator-Baby Side Shows" in *Pediatrics* in August 1979):

"…to call the highly polished metal machines, elaborately fitted with ventilating devices and holding beribboned infants on dainty pillows, *incubators,* is a misnomer. The babies are not incubated, like the chicken from the egg… They are taken from mothers of low vitality, where the conditions of food and air make their survival quite impossible, placed safe behind plate glass and swathed in delicate flannels and in that way reared into normal babyhood…"

Dr. Couney immigrated to America in 1903 and settled in Coney Island, where he had a baby-incubator exhibit every summer for the next 40 years. He married an Irish nurse. Their daughter, Hildegarde, was born prematurely and spent the first three months of her life in an exhibit incubator. Madame Louise Recht, a Budin-trained nurse who worked with Dr. Couney throughout his career, was the central figure on his staff. Dr Couney was proud that he never took a cent from the parents, but he was hurt by their lack of gratitude. They seldom visited their infants, and when the time came for the babies to go home, he had trouble getting the parents to resume their parental responsibilities. This sounds familiar. In today's newborn intensive care units we occasionally experience this, especially when we have the combination of a quite premature baby who spends months in the unit and unmotivated parents who live far away and either are not interested in visiting or cannot afford to visit often. They do not form the necessary bonds with the baby and are often quite unprepared to take on the responsibilities of parenthood.

Couney exhibited elsewhere in between his summer shows, frequently in Chicago. That was where he was when the Dionne quintuplets were born in 1934. The newspaper mogul William Randolph Hearst proposed flying Couney to Canada so that he could provide an ongoing commentary on the condition of the quintuplets in exchange for expert advice. Couney declined, claiming his duty was to the thirty newborns currently under his care. He also feared the quintuplets would soon die and did not want to be involved in a highly publicized failure. When Couney left Chicago he gave his equipment to Dr. Julius Hess, who later became the leading American expert on prematurity, and donated his ambulance to the city of Chicago.

For the 1939-1940 New York World's Fair, Couney planned a major exhibit. A U-shaped structure was erected at considerable expense. There was a suite for Madame Louise Recht and one for Hildegarde (who now worked for her father), rooms for others on the staff—which included fifteen trained nurses, five wet-nurses with their own nursing infants, as well as a cook and a chauffeur—and a sumptuous apartment for Couney himself. The New York Fair, however, was a financial disaster for Couney. He returned to his Coney Island exhibitions, but soon the number of patients diminished and he closed shop.

I have consulted several references on the history of neonatology for this chapter. One of the most intriguing was by the late pioneering neonatologist Dr. William A. Silverman. He had an interesting comment (*Pediatrics* 1979) regarding this piece of medical history:

"It would be fatuous to attach deep significance to this odd chapter in medical history, especially since the incubator-show phenomenon was largely the result of the activities of one man. But I find it hard to ignore the resemblance between the theatrics of the sideshow exhibits and the dramatic actions in present-day neonatal intensive care units. In both cases, I find a disturbing detachment from reality. Premature termination of pregnancy is so often a signal of serious social dysfunction in the family and in the community. The narrowly focused response to this complex problem is quite unreal when viewed from a perspective, which goes beyond the confines of the special care facility. The feeble infant is plucked up and deposited in a theatre-like setting in which superb technical experts make all-out efforts to support life. And when this has been accomplished successfully, the infant graduates. But no comparable effort is mounted to deal with the enormous problems, which face the graduate at home and in the community. Future historians may look back with some fascination at the tunnel vision in the incubator-show era and in the present day. I can almost hear the comment (in French, of course, since the movement did begin in France): *Plus ça change, plus c'est la meme chose."*

Some things have changed however. After the time of Silverman's writing (1979), most neonatal units established follow-up clinics where high-risk babies are followed for up to five years. These are infants who are deemed to be at high risk for developmental problems or whose home situation or family is less than ideal. Physical therapy, nutritional adjustments, and social service interventions are instituted when needed and to the extent that these services are available in the community.

But Silverman was and is right. In this country we do much too little to ensure that our children grow up healthy. We do too little to cure the ills of society. I sympathize with the people of the pro-life movement who wish to maintain life at all costs, yet I am confounded by the fact that these same people often seem unwilling to invest in children: adequate nutrition and a safe environment for all children, good and affordable childcare, universal healthcare, early childhood education with appropriate learning environments, and access to high-quality continuing education are just a few of the things that would help the United States' coming generations become healthier and more productive citizens. We have a long way to go in providing for our future citizens and thereby for the future of our country.

8. Settling In

Within a year we were settled. Our family had come to love Duluth; the children had adjusted and were doing well in school. Summers in Duluth are beautiful and Lake Superior is a spectacular body of water; with our Danish friends, the Hubners, we came to appreciate sailing and eventually bought a boat with a physician friend. In the cold winters skiing became our family sport.

Before my arrival, the Duluth Clinic pediatric department had done much of the groundwork needed to start an NICU. Neonatal intensive care was a new field. In Minnesota, only the University of Minnesota had a unit; the Mayo Clinic was just starting theirs. As time went by, and because it fit well with my interests, I began spending more time at the hospital taking care of sick newborns. This also had the added benefit that it took me out of the office and away from aggravating colleagues.

I had arrived in Duluth in 1973. St. Mary's NICU did not become a reality until the late fall of 1975. Meanwhile, I set about beginning to provide neonatal intensive care. I had worked with sick neonates and preemies in Denmark, but often in Duluth it was "learn as you go" for both the hospital and me. In the spring of 1976, we moved into our new unit. In our planning we had projected that we would need nine beds. Each bed station had oxygen, suction, and numerous outlets to power our incubators, bilirubin lights, IV infusion pumps, monitors, and respirators. I gloried in having room for nine babies and in finally having the appropriate equipment with which to care for them. Until then we had been able to care for only two to four newborns at a time, so this was luxury. Our projections for the new unit had been conservative, however, and within a few years we would run out of space.

We had hired a neonatal nurse from the University of Minnesota as head nurse and had sent some of our nurses off for training at established NICUs. I went to frequent conferences on newborn intensive care, read voraciously the available literature, and spent time at the University of Minnesota's NICU, whose neonatologist had helped develop our unit. Our head nurse developed protocols, trained our nursing staff, and slowly but surely we were up and running.

The pediatricians and I shared taking calls, but I made myself available most of the time to take over patients they admitted to the NICU. Despite some of the pediatricians not appreciating my unavailability one evening a week, Wednesday nights during the summer were my time out for sailing, a pastime that would become a passion.

As our unit began to function as a level III NICU, there were many challenges, and one of them concerned providing adequate nutrition to patients during times of stress. As I helped increasingly smaller infants survive—and at that time babies of two to three pounds were considered very small—I needed to find ways of supporting them nutritionally when they could not feed by mouth. Many premature, and some full-term infants run into problems that make them unable to tolerate oral nutrition for a time. Because babies do not tolerate being without nourishment for long, the alternative is to use intravenous nutrition—hyper alimentation or "hyperal" as we called it—to carry them through. This presents the interesting challenge not only of finding lasting infusion sites but also of developing the right formula for the "hyperal." Adults have standard formulations for IV nutrition, but the formulations for infants must be individualized according to gestation, weight, and chemical and fluid balance.

Creating lasting infusion sites was the first step. Infusing the solution into peripheral veins was not possible; the hypertonic solution would corrode and break down the small peripheral vessels. The solution needed to be released into the bloodstream of a larger vessel where rapid blood-flow ensured quick dilution. I had read in a journal how this was approached at a hospital in Britain. There, the physicians inserted a catheter made of very thin silastic tubing into one of the baby's tiny peripheral veins, threading the catheter through the veins until it reached the large superior vena cava, where the hypertonic solution could be released without causing damage. After some searching, St. Mary's found a place to buy this tubing and ordered it. I had only just received the tubing when one of my preemies, Jonathan, developed necrotizing enterocolitis, a disorder where a transient decrease in blood flow to the gut causes ischemia, and demands that feedings be withheld until the intestine heals. I told Jonathan's parents that it would be difficult for his gut to heal without a steady intake of fluids and calories, including protein, given intravenously. I told them what I intended to do and also that I had never done this before. The parents were anxious, but consented. Without cutting the skin I advanced the very pliable, noodle-like, and thread-thin catheter through an 18-gauge needle into a vein on the inside of the elbow, and advanced it into the superior vena cava, verifying its position by injecting dye through it while taking an x-ray. This first time the tubing easily found its way and everything was perfect. Later I found that placing this catheter could be tricky. The tubing could easily take a wrong turn and wind its way into the neck vein, but usually with some manipulation one could get it into the correct site. Once found to be in the right position, it could stay in place for many weeks at a time, usually until the gut had healed and the baby was able to feed by mouth. In this way, St. Mary's became one of the first places in the U.S., I believe, to use percutaneous intravenous lines (PICC lines) in the newborn, a procedure that is now used in most NICUs across the country.

Jonathan was one of my first preemies. He survived. He was followed closely after discharge and was found to have cerebral palsy. He might have had an intracranial bleed, though I don't remember that now. At the time we had ultrasounds, but not CT scans, to help in diagnosing a bleed. He had great parents who worked hard with him. Despite physical therapy, he did end up in a wheelchair, and in his teens he went to live in a group home where he died when he was in his twenties. Preemies are prone to intracranial bleeds. As neonatology has progressed we have learned what helps prevent them, and we see fewer and fewer children with Jonathan's problems.

The pediatric department had begun looking for a director for the unit before it was up running, and in August of 1976 Dr. Rod Krueger joined me after finishing his fellowship in neonatology. I was not qualified for the directorship because I had not gone through a fellowship in neonatology, and had no board certification. However, since neonatology was such a new subspecialty I was eligible to be grandfathered into the subspecialty by taking the neonatology boards after five years of practice.

I remember Rod interviewing for the position and visiting the NICU in the winter of 1975/1976. I also remember proudly showing him Jonathan and his percutaneous central line. I found it exciting to be able to discuss my patients with a colleague who truly understood the challenges of neonatology. That is what I had treasured in my training and what I had missed since coming to Duluth as none of the pediatricians had much experience or interest in neonatology. So far I had been alone and had made decisions about patients based on what I knew. Now I would have another's perspective to help guide me.

Rod would be the director and manage administrative matters, which suited me fine at the time. I had enough on my plate with a consuming job, three children, and a husband who was also a physician. There were many responsibilities attached to becoming a regional NICU, such as the development of outreach to regional hospitals to teach physicians to care for and stabilize sick newborns and to encourage them to refer those babies to the NICU, as well as developing the transportation system. Therefore it was important to have Rod join me, as one person could not handle all these various duties including patient care. As it turned out, I might have been the one to have started the first NICU north of the Twin Cities, but Rod made it what it became: a truly regional center for neonatal care.

At this time the CEO of St. Mary's Hospital was a nun called Sister Mary Belle Leick, a masculine, corporate woman who did her networking on the golf course with the men and drank with the best of them. She had somewhat old-fashioned attitudes, however, and refused to let female nurses wear pants, at the same time checking that dresses were long enough by having the wearers bend over. She was very parsimonious and sometimes the hospital had whole lengths of walls painted the same ugly color because she had found a great deal on a particular paint.

One day I received a call from her, "I've noticed that you are not keeping up on your discharge summaries. How come?" she asked.

Summaries of a patient's hospital stay go to the patient's home physician and should ideally be dictated at the time of discharge. Like many others, I tended to procrastinate on my summaries until I had some uninterrupted time. The often complicated and long hospital stays of my patients meant that it took me quite some time to sort out the course of a patient's illness and fashion it into a comprehensive narrative. Though this was no excuse, it should not have been the concern of the CEO.

"Well, I guess there is a lot of demand on my time," was my answer.

"Has it occurred to you that maybe, as a wife and mother, you should not be practicing medicine?"

Wow! Not only did my colleagues treat me to unsuitable remarks—but to hear this from a woman! I took a deep breath while I contemplated an appropriate reply to this inappropriate question, but in the end I just hung up on her. A cop-out? Definitely! But diplomacy was not my strong suit and words might have been said that I most certainly would have regretted.

When the unit first opened we had hired a small group of older nurses and a larger group of young nurses straight out of nurses' training—many of the latter would make neonatology their lifetime career. The older nurses quickly decided that they would call me by my first name. I had always been called Dr. Aas and felt it proper that I should be addressed that way. I had, after all, worked hard to attain the M.D. degree. It quickly became apparent, however, that I would be working in close contact with the nurses—how close we didn't know until the unit was filled to overflowing! Being on a first name basis helped create a sense of camaraderie as we worked toward the common goal of improving care for sick newborns. We were in this together, and we needed to be able to trust and rely on each other in order to create the teamwork that is so important for good care. Besides, nurses were usually called by their first names, except when they were supervisors. Why should I be calling them Sandy, Barb or Debbie, while refusing to allow them to call me Martha? Mostly we were contemporaries and it only made sense that we should be on a first name basis. I therefore swallowed my pride. I am not sure this would have happened if the unit had been started by a male physician, but when Rod came on board he was given no choice. He was "Rod" from the get-go.

Sometimes I felt the nurses were almost part of my family. They knew my husband and children and I, to a certain extent, knew theirs. When my daughter was in elementary school, I often took her to work with me on weekends if I expected to finish my rounds quickly. She was set up at the only table in the unit with paper and crayons. She was fairly patient as I focused on seeing the patients—I was generally efficient in making rounds and refrained from small talk until I was done—but at times Christine would say, "Mom, when can we go?" When a call for transport or a high-risk delivery made it evident I would not be able to take her home any time soon, I called Hans to pick her up.

After Rod joined me the two of us shared taking calls. On a given day, the one on call saw her own patients, but also dealt with all the emergencies: babies being born and transports, and continued to do that through the whole twenty-four hours, while the other just saw his own patients. The next day the tables were turned. We alternated weekends with one of us being on call Friday-Saturday-Sunday—seventy-two hours. It was a tough schedule that we lived with for four years until our third neonatologist, Dr. Soo Young Pi, joined us.

When busy at night, I stayed in the unit. During lulls I tried to catch some sleep in our small family conference room, curling up on a small three-seat vinyl outdoor couch in my scrubs. This small conference room and the head nurse's office were the only spaces we had outside the unit. Looking back I realize how cramped it was; we had so little room. The nurses loved to come in and wake me when they needed me, watching me first fight my way out of sleep and then try to straighten my disarrayed hair (how I sometimes wished I had a butch cut! there is no glamour in being a hardworking physician). To her glee, one of the nurses once found me with a piece of gum stuck in my hair, something she has never let me forget. She helpfully removed the gum with scissors. Later in the life of the NICU, the nurses took to doing skits at the Christmas party where they poked fun at us doctors and at themselves. None of our idiosyncrasies escaped their notice.

The NICU was right next to the obstetrical service and the delivery rooms. This was when women labored in labor rooms and were moved to a delivery room when the time came. The delivery room was set up with all the instruments and equipment needed for vaginal deliveries. If a Caesarian section was needed, however, the mother had to be moved once again to the floor below for surgery. This was not the best setup for a woman in the throes of labor, but it was typical of its time. Later we would move to a birthing center, where the mother labored and delivered the baby in the same room. Should a C-section become necessary it was done on the same floor.

During those years when we were building up the unit, the obstetricians and the neonatologists collaborated in outreach to regional hospitals. We taught local physicians about resuscitation and stabilization of newborns and taught them when it was appropriate to call us for transport to the NICU. By this time our neonatal transport service was up and running, and we were always ready to go where we were needed by ambulance.

However, it is preferable to have a high-risk mother deliver in a hospital with an NICU; precious time is lost in the transfer of a sick baby, and this time could mean the difference between life and death. Over the years, most regional physicians responded. They became very capable at dealing with a sick newborn until we could transfer the baby and became much more likely in case of an anticipated high-risk delivery to transfer the undelivered mother to our institution where one of us neonatologists could be in attendance at the delivery. We attended all high-risk deliveries and C-sections.

III. The Babies

9. Growing Pains

The most glorious moments in your life are not the so-called days of success, but rather those days when out of dejection and despair you feel rising in you a challenge, to life, and the promise of future accomplishments.

Gustave Flaubert

And so we settled into hard work and time passed quickly. With a nine-bed unit we had underestimated the need for newborn intensive care in our region, which covered the western part of the Upper Peninsula of Michigan, northwestern Wisconsin, and northeastern Minnesota. A census of six patients quickly grew to nine, then to fifteen and occasionally topping eighteen. We did not turn any patients away. We accepted everyone, and we received the whole range of neonatology, though we transferred babies with congenital cardiac malformations to the University of Minnesota or Minneapolis Children's Hospital. Soon I had spent close to six years in the field of neonatology.

In the fall of 1979, Hans was hospitalized in the intensive care unit with a spontaneous pneumothorax: a hole had blown in his lungs and air had escaped to the surrounding thoracic space for no apparent reason. He might have incurred it while clearing rock on our newly-acquired land where he planned to start a berry farm.

It became a time of much worry. Air kept accumulating and several more chest tubes were put in. A diagnosis of tuberculosis was entertained, but not proven. I worked every day, and brought Peter and Christine to see Hans whenever I could. Both were distraught by their father's pale appearance and by the tubes in his nose, arms, and chest.

During the following ten days, I was glad the children were older. We had always lived on the edge as far as managing the home front, and this almost pushed us over it. With the neonatal unit growing so rapidly, and Rod and I being on call every other day, I was gone from home a lot. This was a demanding schedule for anyone, let alone a wife and mother. Hans was home more than I was, as he was less busy at that point in his career, and he was good at getting food on the table and keeping the kitchen clean, but there was always laundry piling up, not to mention messy kids' rooms, which I managed to ignore.

Michael, nineteen, had left the nest. He had graduated from high school the year before and had spent a year in Europe before beginning school at Macalester College. He had departed from Duluth on an ocean-going merchant vessel, leaving a void in our home. I wondered where the time had gone, and how he could have grown up so fast. I felt the years had flown, and I mourned that I never seemed to be able to dwell in the moment, feeling its full intensity, attuned to every little change in my children. They had grown while I wasn't watching.

Shortly before Hans's illness, I had decided we no longer needed domestic help. For quite a few years we had Rachel, who was at the house every day when the children returned from school and stayed until one of us came home from work. Now, with Hans ill, a lot of the burden shifted onto the kids. So now it was time for everyone to help with chores. We coped, and eventually Hans was discharged, ten pounds skinnier, his lungs healed. Thankfully there was no underlying disease to explain the pneumothorax.

Having practiced neonatology for more than five years, I now qualified to sit for the Boards in Neonatology. I had read extensively, attended many courses in my rapidly evolving field, and was now preparing to take those exams. I studied night and day, any time I had. Six years of apprenticeship, six years of working with neonates, six years of learning: reckoning day—the Boards—was arriving. While working and being on call every other day for five years, my brain had soaked up knowledge and now the examination was a month-and-a-half away.

I had a week's review course scheduled in Chicago. It happened to be just as Hans came out of the hospital. He knew the course was important for me and assured me he could manage alone, and he did. I felt guilty for not being there for him when he needed me and had the illusion he couldn't possibly recover without me. But when I returned, thanks to the help of the kids and of our friends the Hubners, he was doing just fine and was ready to go back to work.

The stress continued, however. Peter's confirmation ceremony was coming up and we were expecting a visit from Hans's parents and his aunt. They arrived, the house bustled with people, the Boards were still ahead of me, but I could not cram any more into my brain. Instead I concentrated on my work and on our guests, Fie, Richard, and aunt Anna, making short trips with them as they learned more about Minnesota and Wisconsin.

Then Jørgen and Lisbeth, our Danish friends from our internship days in Kansas City, announced they were in the U.S. for a conference. Could they visit…? Just for a few days? They ended up staying for the confirmation as well, and the Hubners across the street graciously put them up.

Our house on Rockview Court was filled to bursting. Our small nuclear family, so long without relatives, gained life. The pneumothorax, our work, the studying were all forgotten in this flurry of activity with Danish spoken in every nook and cranny. Hans felt good and drew strength from his family's visit. The children also grew in the knowledge that extended family was important.

Afterwards, all became quiet again. I left for the exams in Chicago and arrived at the hotel where the Boards were to take place. The next morning I sat in a room full of eager young physicians—all much younger than me—worked at multiple-choice-questions that were surprisingly reasonable—no trick questions—and was thankful when it was over. How I got through that intense day I really don't know, because I seemed to have no energy left. Yet, you can put in a herculean effort for a short time before you collapse.

And collapse I did! I was deeply fatigued for months. I functioned at work only because I had to. When I came home I was exhausted. My family bore it with grace. Hans was supportive and helpful. Christine was a little mother to me, comforting me with hugs, working hard to cheer me up. Even Peter, though now decidedly more grown up, hugged me at times. I also was depressed and failed to easily snap back to my former energy level.

I was grateful to have a terrific family to sustain me, though I felt a burden to them when I was depressed. Depression had shadowed me since my adolescence. Mostly I functioned despite it, but sometimes not. Yet I could not give up my job, because I knew bouts of depression would afflict me even more often if I didn't work, and I would be a worse mother. That was my reality. Somehow we all made it through this time.

Meanwhile I realized the importance of exercise for one's sense of wellbeing. It is surprising it took me so long to figure that out. I had never engaged in exercise for its own sake. As a child and young person I had not been involved in sports. Since living in Duluth I had skied in the wintertime with my family for the fun of it. But now I needed to do something to keep my body in shape and to generate energy. I was tentative as I started running. I was forty-two and running did not come naturally to me. I increased my mileage by fractions, and eventually got to a point where I was able to get into a routine of doing my much-needed workouts. Slowly but surely the depression lifted as my body was re-energized.

10. Jimmy from Canada

What is life? It is the flash of a firefly in the night. It is the breath of a buffalo in the wintertime. It is the little shadow, which runs across the grass and loses itself in the sunset.

Blackfoot Saying

In the twenty-three years I worked at St. Mary's Medical Center, my work environment was the NICU, Labor and Delivery, and surgery. Only rarely did I visit other floors of the hospital in a professional capacity. Exceptions were if a mother was hospitalized in a specialized unit or when a newborn or a young infant was brought to the ER in severe distress. A call from the ER most often meant a dire situation.

Thus it was on a June morning thirty or more years ago when the emergency room called us about Jimmy. One of our nurses, Sandy, and I sprinted down the stairs to the first floor, ran down the hallway to the ER where nurses quickly directed us to the room. On the examining table lay a large, bluish-pale baby. A respiratory therapist was ventilating him with a bag and mask while the emergency room physician was readying to intubate him. Before getting any information at all I took over for the ER doc and intubated the baby with a 3.5 ET-tube.

"He arrested when he arrived. We were able to give intracardiac epi and he now has a heart rate," the ER doctor said. "Otherwise we know little about him." As I was ventilating him on the ET-tube, his heart rate came up. But though his lips and nail beds were gaining some pinkness, his skin remained very pale and blue. I examined him and noticed a shock of black hair, unmistakable American Indian features, and a well-nourished state. His lungs had the râles—crackles—heard with pneumonia, but otherwise the most obvious clinical feature was that he appeared to be in hypovolemic shock: little blood was going to the surface of his body and this lent his skin the pale-bluish, in places mottled, hue. His extremities were cold, his skin slightly clammy. For whatever reason, he had either lost a lot of fluids or was in septic shock. The body reacts to this decrease in circulating blood volume by shutting down the circulation to the skin and directing blood to vital areas, such as brain, heart, lungs, and kidneys. He needed fluids and pressors quickly.

With me in the room was the ER doctor, the emergency room nurses, Sandy, and the respiratory therapist to whom I now handed off the ventilation. Each of us began examining one or the other of his extremities for likely veins, finding none. Veins are hard to find in a well-nourished infant. The fact that little blood was going to the skin did not help matters. I quickly shaved his beautiful hair on one side of his head and was able to see a vein, where I placed a twenty-three-gauge Jelco catheter. We started running a solution of dextrose and normal saline at a rapid rate for his size. Then I drew an arterial sample of blood from his radial artery to be sent for blood gases, CBC, diff, electrolytes, and blood culture. I did a spinal tap and a supra-pubic bladder tap, and got him started on antibiotics. Then we moved him to the NICU in a transport incubator so he would stay warm.

All this time I had no history of what had been going on with Jimmy. The most important goal right now was to stabilize him. While we were connecting the endotracheal tube in his trachea to the respirator, Sandy told me his parents had been brought to the NICU. I asked that they come to the bedside. They were obviously very concerned. They said they were from north of Thunder Bay in Ontario, Canada, and that they had been on vacation in Minnesota, visiting friends in the Mille Lacs area. Jimmy was three weeks old and had weighed nine pounds at birth. He had been doing well and gaining weight until this present illness. He had begun having some diarrhea in Mille Lacs, was a little lethargic and was not nursing well. They therefore decided to head home. But as they got ready to leave that morning, they noticed that his respirations had become rapid with long pauses in between. Hence they went to the nearest hospital, in Sandstone, which sent him to us by ambulance.

All the while I was acutely aware that his blood pressure was low. We needed to start pressors and monitor his central venous pressure. In newborns, the umbilical vessels provide the best route for monitoring pressures and administering fluids, but Jimmy was now three weeks old. Often when babies are this age, the umbilical vessels have closed but occasionally it is possible to get venous access this way.

While Sandy restrained the baby I began cleaning off the umbilical area with Betadine and alcohol. Thereafter I covered the surrounding area with sterile drapes. The cord had fallen off, but at the bottom of the navel I could clearly discern the three vessels, the two round thick-walled arteries and the single umbilical vein that usually appears as a larger slit with a thin vessel wall. I was able to dilate the umbilical vein with a curved forceps and insert a catheter that miraculously advanced until blood returned. An x-ray assured me that the catheter was in the inferior vena cava through which we could now monitor his central venous pressure and infuse fluids.

Throughout the day we calibrated his fluids according to his electrolytes and pressures and tried to combat his mixed respiratory and metabolic acidosis. He was putting out urine, but not much. We struggled all day to get his pressures up. I felt his vascular collapse was as much due to sepsis as to fluid loss from the diarrhea, which by history had been less than fulminant.

Jimmy kept me so busy that I had little time for the parents. I could not sit down with them in privacy to talk about what was going on. I had to communicate my thoughts while I was busy at his bedside. The social worker was present, and she and Sandy talked with them as well. As time passed, however, and we saw no improvement, I let the parents know that the outlook was not good: it was taking a long time to turn him around, and there was a possibility that he might not survive.

This was tough news for parents who the day before had had a healthy baby already three weeks old. I suspected late onset group B streptococcal sepsis, which is an infection contracted from the carrier mother, and which can manifest itself at birth in the so-called early onset, which is often fulminant and fatal. The late onset, occurring several weeks after birth, is usually less severe, but can be fatal as well.

Jimmy was admitted to the NICU, where working conditions now had become difficult because it was so crowded. In the five years since we had opened the unit in 1976, it had grown exponentially and there were plans for a new unit. The small unit designed for nine babies contained a small table for charting. Surrounding it were twelve to fifteen isolettes.

There were cords, extension cords, power strips, monitors, respirators, and bili-lights everywhere. There was hardly room to have the parents by the bedside. In retrospect it seems incredible that we could function there. To get Jimmy's chest-x-ray, isolettes, table, and chairs had to be moved. His chest-x-ray showed a severe pneumonia with almost complete opacification, which made ventilation difficult.

I felt exhausted, as did the nurses working with me, not just from the physical work, but also from the frustration that nothing we did seemed to make a difference. Sandy, who was assigned to Jimmy, had long since recruited another nurse to help her; she could hardly keep up with the many orders. He stabilized somewhat over the next several days though his lungs were still in terrible shape. His kidney function worsened, however, and his poor neurologic status underscored the fact that he had suffered severe brain malfunction, probably around his cardiac arrest.

Several days later Jimmy died. Losing a baby is hard for everyone involved, primarily for the parents, of course, but also for the staff. It is especially hard losing a large, previously healthy baby. The parents were bewildered as they contemplated how fast he went downhill, and the mother was unable to accept his death as she sat cradling his body. Sandy and I talked to them about the need to contact a funeral home. The parents were adamant they just wanted to take the baby home themselves—"right now," they said—and have the appropriate Indian ceremony and burial at home.

When I first thought back to Jimmy's case, my recollection was that Jimmy was placed in the arms of his mother and sent off. When they crossed the border into Canada the border guards would see Jimmy, one hoped, as a live baby asleep in his mother's arms. This was long before 9/11 and the border crossing into Canada was fairly lax. Certainly one did not need to show passports, just proof of residency. I assumed they would have been waved through, and that the parents would have brought Jimmy home without any hassles.

As I write this, however, I become aware that if the above scenario is indeed true, then we did something illegal. There are laws prohibiting carrying a body across state lines, and crossing an international border is an even bigger issue. The hospital would not have let us send him home without the proper papers. I become determined to clear this up.

I call Kathy McQuinn, a social worker who has worked at Duluth hospitals for the past thirty-plus years, to ask her if she knows who the social worker was in the NICU at the time of Jimmy's hospitalization. "I was," she says, "and yes, I remember Jimmy. How could I forget? It was such an unusual situation." I marvel at her recall.

Jimmy died on a Sunday, Kathy tells me, on a Fourth of July weekend. She was on call and after Jimmy's death I had asked her to come to the hospital to help take care of the family and get them on their way, as I had been called out on a transport (this explains my poor recall). And yes, she said, bodies cannot be transported across state lines without proper certification from the hospital and from a funeral home.

Because the mother refused to leave Jimmy after he died, Kathy took the father and two other men, family members, to the lobby of the hospital where they could have privacy to talk. The men were very jovial and talkative, displaying a great sense of humor at this somber time, Kathy remembers. They were Cree Indians, they said, and their custom was to keep the body of a deceased in the home for four days after death to allow the spirit a chance to get back into the body. Because of this they were opposed to embalming.

Kathy wondered how she was going to get the family home without violating their beliefs and without violating Minnesota state laws. She called the funeral home across the street from the hospital and learned that the body, indeed, needed to be embalmed. But Kathy was able to convince the funeral director, and this is a testament to her skills, to put embalming fluid only on the skin of the baby. This was acceptable to the family.

As the mother and baby came down to the lobby in preparation for leaving, Kathy realized that if she sent the family alone to the funeral home, they might just get in their car and head for Thunder Bay. They would do anything to escape what could, to them, have seemed like a hostage situation. So, she accompanied them to the funeral home where embalming fluid was applied to the skin of the baby, the appropriate papers were filled out, and a certificate given to the parents. All formalities were taken care of.

The mother took the baby in her arms and the family got into the car and drove north. Kathy and I are both sure the parents would not have revealed to the border guards that Jimmy was dead. To do so, they would have felt, would have exposed them to undue scrutiny and the risk of being detained once again. Jimmy was just a baby asleep in his mother's arms.

That the mother could hold him in her arms on the way home hopefully helped her in her grief. Did the spirit find its way back? If so, Jimmy had one persistent spirit. It had already left the body once in the emergency room and had returned.

11. Forest Breeze

His name is what sticks with me. His parents gave it to him for reasons I know nothing about. To me, his clinical course has long been forgotten as he was my colleague Rod's patient, but I knew then that he was a survivor and had been right from the start. I like to think of how scrappy he was, a fighter, fighting against all odds in an inhospitable world: he had been born prematurely in the north woods of Minnesota in the midst of winter. From what little I know this is how I imagine his beginnings—before he came to us in the NICU.

Leslie clutches her tiny baby. Languidly, she settles back against the pillows her husband, Jess, has shored up around her. She has just given birth—to both child and placenta. The baby is tiny, his skin red and slightly translucent, his body scrawny with little fat.

"So, how far along do we figure I was?" she asks her husband.

"Well…I don't remember what the doctor said. Didn't we get pregnant back in June?"

She thinks this over for a while.

"Seven-and-a-half months then…about 30 weeks," she says. "Oh, he is so tiny, he can't possibly survive, can he?"

"I'm sure he's tough," he says, though when he looks at the baby he doubts that this is true.

"What're we going to do?"

He doesn't answer. What can they do? They live so far from anybody and the snow has been coming down all afternoon and evening; already three feet have piled up. Even if they had a phone, nobody can get to them now. He can't carry Leslie and the baby out to the car a mile-and-a-half away.

"I'll keep him right next to the skin on my breast and cover us up with blankets to keep him warm,"—instinctively she knows that if he gets cold he will die—"and we must keep the wood stove hot." She smiles and tries to look confident.

Then she lies back with the baby stretched out on his stomach on her chest, his head touching her chin. He is breathing and she can feel his small heart beating. She positions his head to one side, so his nose is uncovered. It is just unreal, she thinks, that I should have this baby so early and so quickly. While sweeping the floors in the afternoon, she thought she had contractions, but Jess was gone in the woods and there was no way of letting anyone know. When Jess got home, the contractions increased and she knew for sure she was in labor. His breathing is so quiet, she thinks, like a gentle wind in the top of the trees. She dozes off, conscious all the time of the little creature who depends on her for warmth. She had not been in labor long before he was born.

Jess goes outside to chop more wood. That is the one thing they have enough of: many downed trees lie scattered in the forest around the cabin. He had worried about the pregnancy, but Leslie had said, "There is nothing more natural than having a baby. People have babies all the time. They had them in the Stone Ages, they had them in the Middle Ages, they had them in the field while tilling the land, and after delivering the babies the women got up and went on with their work. I'm healthy and I'll have a healthy baby. We'll do fine. Nothing to it."

That might have been true. But they have no health care, and little money. Leslie tends bar, and he works for a construction company, when there is work that is, and they make it okay. A healthy baby might not have been much of a problem. But this premature baby is a problem, one way or another. He fears the baby will die. Then they'll have to think about a funeral; but that could be simple. Jess had looked forward to a healthy little boy, one who would grow up with them here in the woods. But that is not to be. They are renting this cabin for the time being, but they hope eventually to have their own house somewhere around here, a house he will build.

He thinks about keeping the baby warm in this weather. They should all be able to stay warm enough as long as he keeps the wood stove going. He carries in the wood and heaps it next to the stove. Leslie is sleeping, it seems. He peeks under the down blanket and sees the tiny body moving a little. The baby stretches out an arm whose fingers he gently touches. How red he is. He places his finger under the baby's palm and the baby grasps his finger. "Does he know who I am?" Jess asks himself. He talks quietly to the baby, who seems to squeeze his finger a little harder. Maybe he does know my voice, he thinks. He feels a sudden tenderness for the baby. If only he could live.

Leslie wakes up and finds that the baby accidentally has found his own fingers and is sucking hard on them. She feels milk oozing from her breast. Somehow I've got to feed him, she thinks. She puts the baby to her breast, but the nipple is too big for his small mouth, yet he keeps searching for something to latch on to. She tries to position herself so she can squeeze her breast and let the drops drip into his mouth. He seems to like that. He swallows the drops, looking for more. How can I possibly get enough into him? she thinks. What does he need, a couple of ounces? She has no idea. But he is warm and vigorous, which is a good thing, isn't it? She keeps squeezing her breast. Thick colostrum drips into the baby's mouth. Who are you? Leslie asks him quietly. You should have a name.

"Jess, what should we call him?"

"Do we have to call him anything yet?" *As he says this Jess wonders why he doesn't want to think about a name. A name would make him a person, a real baby...their son!*

"Of course he should have a name. You know, I have an idea—his breathing is like a soft breeze in the trees. Why don't we call him Forest Breeze? What do you think?"

"Forest Breeze? That's silly, Leslie."

"Why? We can call him anything we want, and that's what I would like. He sounds like a soft forest breeze."

"Well, I suppose...American Indians name themselves for things in nature."

"Yes, they do, don't they?"

"All right," *Jess says, dropping down next to the bed, smiling at Leslie and then at his son,* "we'll call him Forest Breeze—strange name, eh?"

"I think he likes it," *Leslie says.* "He looks so content."

The storm continued to rage outside and drifts piled up in front of the door. Every half hour or so, Jess went outside to shovel free the entryway, but eventually he went to bed and some time during the night he felt the wind dying down. Leslie woke up about every half hour to check on the baby to make sure he was warm and to feed him. She had no idea how much he was getting. It didn't seem like enough, but he was content.

In the morning she got up and found a cardboard box that she lined with warm blankets. Fortunately she had some baby clothes she dressed the baby in, though they were way too big. She placed him in the cardboard box, wrapped in blankets. Next to the stove was an alcove where they kept the firewood. In this warm spot she put the box. As the day wore on she started feeling stronger and more confident that the baby was getting some nutrition. Maybe we'll do OK, she thought, maybe he will get stronger and be able to feed from my breast. Jess was busy shoveling outside and she could see he was trying to tamp down a path toward the road.

The next morning, as she was tending to the baby on the table in the living room that was filled with sunlight, she noticed that his color had changed. He was a little yellow. Even the whites of his eyes were yellow. Jaundice, she thought. She knew he might need to be exposed to light. The sun shines on her bed in the morning, warming it. The midwife she had talked to had said that was how one could treat jaundice in a baby, by placing it naked in the sun, but she knew he would not stay warm there. He was too little. He would catch cold. He also seemed less active, a little lethargic even, this morning. He was doing less rooting when she held him near her breast. She knew they had to do something…but what? How could they take him out in twenty-below-zero weather?

She resolved that something needed to happen. When Jess came in with more firewood she said, "We must take the baby to the hospital. He's not doing well."

Jess said nothing. He just felt the fear. He had known this all along: the baby would not survive. But he couldn't tell Leslie that.

"How are we going to get to the car?" he asked.

"I think I can walk there."

"But the baby…what are we going to do about him? He'll freeze to death." Not just a figure of speech, Jess thought.

"I'll bundle him up. Put him inside my jacket, keep him on my chest, he should stay warm." She wasn't at all sure about this, but felt a need to sound confident.

All of a sudden she remembered the snowshoes.

"Oh, Jess, we have the snowshoes. It'll be so much easier if I can use the snowshoes."

"Oh, absolutely. But before we do anything, I want to put on my own snowshoes and walk out to the car and start it up, so it can be warm for you,"

Jess said. "I don't want you and the little guy out there unless I know the car will start."

When Jess returned—the car had started right away—she managed somehow with his help to get the snowshoes on while she and Forest Breeze were bundled up in an oversized parka of Jess's. Leslie had tied him to herself with a large scarf around her bosom, so he wouldn't slide down inside the parka. He was lying between her breasts. As they made their way, Leslie stopped frequently to make sure Forest Breeze could breathe. The hat she had put on his head tended to fall down over his nose.

And somehow...they made it to the car, which was warm now, and they set out for the thirty-five-mile drive to International Falls Hospital. Leslie lay back in her seat and opened the parka a little. There he was, breathing quietly, her little boy! The trip seemed interminable. Would he continue to be okay?

Once at the hospital, she carefully slid out of the car and walked into the emergency room. She opened her parka wide, and eased the tiny baby out of the scarf.

"Here is Forest Breeze," she said, relieved that they had arrived safely, giving the warm, living bundle over to the astonished nurses. As they unbundled him he opened his eyes, stretched, and grimaced as if in a smile.

My colleague Rod Krueger remembers receiving a call from International Falls about Forest Breeze. When he and the team got there by ambulance and went to pick up the baby in the nursery, the parents had left the hospital. Forest Breeze was taken to the NICU, but the parents, when they returned to International Falls Hospital, were upset that he had been transferred since they had already brought him to "a hospital." Rod remembers them as "flower children" from California who had moved to northern Minnesota to live in the wilderness and grow things. Nonetheless, Forest Breeze did amazingly well despite weighing only somewhere around two pounds. His mother came to stay in the NICU and provided him with breast milk. He grew quickly and was discharged home when his weight had reached five pounds.

The family wasn't heard from for a couple of years. Then the NICU received a message written on birch bark that Forest Breeze was doing well. Five years later the information somehow filtered back to the NICU that the parents had given up on Minnesota and moved back to California.

Forest Breeze remains for me the baby with the enormous will to live.

12. A Heartache

The day in 1982, when seven-year-old Walter, the very first surviving small preemie in my time at the hospital and maybe in the hospital's entire history, cut the tape and opened the new and much larger neonatal intensive care unit, was the fulfillment of a dream. When our statistics showed that we consistently had thirteen to fifteen babies in a unit built for nine, plans had been drawn up for a larger facility. Today I think about how excited we were to have room for twenty-five babies, to have a place with so many outlets that we no longer needed to worry about stumbling over extension cords and power strips, with each baby having her own little station where all her necessities were kept in drawers, with respirators and monitors placed accessibly. Yet now—in 2013—this second unit has also outgrown its usefulness and is about to be replaced with a third unit where, in a complete departure in concept, there are individual rooms for each baby and his family. Times change, and we have learned new things about nursing care that allow babies to thrive better. The 2013 unit will reflect that.

But in 1982, our new facility was state of the art for its time. The young boy, Walter, who cut the ribbon that day, had been born in 1975. He weighed 1000 grams (two pounds four ounces) at birth, had no respiratory problems, tolerated his feedings, and basically just grew and grew until he was discharged from the hospital. He was the child of older parents, his father worked at the hospital, and it was a natural that he should be our poster child.

In the new unit, long counters separated rows of incubator stations. The sun streamed through the windows to the east, the unit's brightness a contrast to the first unit that had no windows. It was light and airy and all three of us, Soo Young, Rod and I, as well as our staff, were looking forward to working there. Dr. Soo Young Pi had joined us just two years before. A very knowledgeable physician, he was a great addition to our staff. He stayed with us for fifteen years until he left to start the first Neonatal Intensive Care Unit in Korea at Seoul University and became the grandfather of neonatology in that country.

One of my first patients in the new unit was Jason, a child I would never forget. Never had I ached for parents the way I ached for this mother and father. Yet, though Jason's case was heart wrenching, I remember only snippets of his story. For weeks he was my nightmare. This happened so long ago. Is that why I remember so little? Or have I deliberately erased the memories from my mind? Maybe. Sometimes memories become too painful and are sublimated. What I do know is that this happened well before close monitoring of mothers for gestational diabetes became routine.

Jason was born at a small hospital in our referral area and weighed eleven pounds at birth. He was eagerly awaited and when the parents heard the weight estimates, they were amazed that they should have produced so large a child; neither of them was tall or heavy. A Caesarian section was done for failure of the mother's labor to progress.

Some hours after delivery Jason's breathing became rapid and labored, he turned pale and jittery, and eventually had what appeared to be a seizure for which he was given phenobarbital. A low blood sugar seemed to explain all the symptoms. After being fed glucose water by mouth he seemed better, and the blood sugar improved for a while only to plunge again.

In retrospect, it was clear that Jason had presented as an infant of a diabetic mother, and that he was especially big because the mother's gestational diabetes had not been recognized and treated. In untreated diabetes, the mother's high blood sugar is transferred across the placenta to the baby. Unlike the mother, the baby is able to respond to the high blood sugar level by putting out more insulin from his intact pancreas. The sugar is converted into fat and the baby becomes obese. The insulin production, however, is not easily switched off at birth when the cutting of the cord prevents further flow of sugar from the mother. The baby's blood sugar therefore drops dramatically within hours of birth. Besides problems with blood sugar, these babies also have an increased risk of respiratory distress and congenital anomalies of heart, central nervous system, and urinary tracts.

When Jason's blood sugar again plummeted, it was now to a level that urgently needed treatment with intravenous sugar. The attending physician was called. Because of the baby's obesity he was unable to find a peripheral vein, and as there was some urgency about raising the blood sugar, he quickly placed an umbilical artery catheter giving a bolus of 20 percent glucose. The blood sugar improved, and he followed the bolus with a constant drip of 10 percent glucose through the umbilical vessel. Vital signs became stable and there was no more seizure-like activity.

I don't know when the nurses noticed this, but at one point in time they became aware that Jason's right leg was pale and mottled. The physician was again called. He reviewed the x-ray of the arterial catheter placement, found the catheter to be in the femoral artery, and pulled back on the catheter. When the leg didn't improve immediately, he pulled the catheter completely, replacing it with an umbilical venous catheter. Then he called our NICU informing us that he would like to transfer the child. Transfer would be via the local ambulance, he said, as the baby was stable.

Jason arrived in our unit a few hours later, brought in by the local EMTs on a stretcher. When I first saw him, he not only had low muscle tone as is characteristic of infants of diabetic mothers, he also looked somewhat obtunded and did not respond to stimuli. His right leg was white and no pulses could be found in that leg. We applied measures to improve the circulation of the leg. On suspicion of a vasospasm in the artery, we put warm blankets around the leg and gave vasodilators. We warmed the opposite leg as well to get a sympathetic reaction. There seemed to be a slight improvement in the color of the leg, or maybe we were deluding ourselves, as we still didn't feel a pulse. In case a clot was a factor, we started anticoagulants to prevent further clotting. Never before had I seen this in a baby (nor would I see it again), and I felt rather desperate when there was no improvement in the circulation.

On examination of this very large and fat baby, I additionally noted that the fontanel was bulging. A lumbar puncture was done and he was put on antibiotics. The spinal tap, however, suggested neither meningitis nor an intracranial bleed. We therefore treated him for brain edema with mannitol, diuretics, and ventilatory support. Surgeons were consulted.

They thought it would be impossible to remove a possible clot in this size patient.

The mother was transferred to our maternity ward and arrived shortly after Jason, her husband accompanying her. Both parents were young, with no other children. While clearly overwhelmed and intimidated by the environment of the NICU, the mother listened intently to what we told her and soon she was able to abstract from all the high tech machines and focus solely on Jason. Because of complications from the C-section, she came to the NICU infrequently during Jason's first days there, but her understanding of his situation grew as time passed. The father was a muscular young construction worker who exuded a subdued masculinity. Like the mother, he said little. With quiet intensity he stood by Jason's bedside, palpably weighed down by his concern for mother and baby.

Because the NICU was filled to capacity and because of an initial suspicion of infection, Jason was kept in an isolation unit. To see him and examine him entailed not only physical effort of a sort—isolation demanded that we don gloves, cap, mask, and gown—but it also required emotional energy. Every day I forced myself to see and examine this full-term baby who should have been screaming, kicking, and feeding. I watched him deteriorate without being able to change the downhill course of his illness. His leg remained white and after a week it began to become necrotic. We again had the surgeons see him, this time to discuss amputation of the leg, but in view of the baby's neurologic status, no one felt inclined to tackle the situation.

The cerebral edema subsided, but still Jason's neurologic status did not improve. He had needed respiratory support from the first day because of inadequate respiratory effort and continued to need that support. We did not feel he was stable enough to be fed by gavage, so we fed him intravenously. Because of his obesity I could access no peripheral veins, but instead made a cut-down on the inside of his elbow where I knew I would find a vein. Once the vein had been located, I nicked it with small sharp scissors and threaded the thin silicone catheter into the superior vena cava, the central vein in his upper chest, and fed parenteral nutrition through it.

We met frequently with the parents to explain what was going on, but where they continuously hoped for good news, there was none. The joy I usually felt at being able to heal a patient was replaced by despondency. I was besieged by powerlessness, as he daily reminded me that I was unable to reverse his condition.

Instead, I felt intense gratitude to the nurses. My already high regard for their work grew into awe. I had always been aware that nurses were the front line soldiers, fielding—and sometimes deflecting—the parents' many questions. While they were often the first to tell the parents the good news, "Your baby tolerated his first feeding," or "Your baby is needing less oxygen," they were also the ones, present at the bedside at all times, to relate to parents when no progress was being made. With rapid worsening of a baby's status the neonatologist always remains close by, but with slow and steady deterioration, not necessarily. The nurses were frequently the main supporters of the parents through their long ordeal. I, as the neonatologist, could remove myself from the situation, but for their eight-hour shift, the nurses could not. I often wondered how they managed it, day after day. Most nurses feel an enormous commitment to their patients, and this was true of our nurses as well. Despite the emotional toll, many stayed with us for decades and they constituted the core of our nursing staff.

Eventually when Jason showed no neurologic progress, we just waited for him to die. We did not take him off the respirator because he still had some respiratory movement, and though his EEG was mostly flat, it is an unreliable indicator in a newborn. We supported him for three weeks until his organs began failing one by one, allowing us to discontinue life support.

The parents remained with him for all this time, and it was a nightmare for them as well. They did not understand where things had gone so wrong and ardently kept hoping for some change in him. When we told them we could do no more for him they just wished, as did we, that he would die soon.

When his heartbeat became slow and feeble we took him off the respirator. All the tubes were removed from him and the nurse had the mother help bathe him and shampoo his hair. Then we watched as the mother dressed him in clothes she had readied for the day she would take him home, and she swathed him in blankets.

"I want to do this real slowly," she whispered, "because this is the only time I get to dress Jason. And the crib I have at home…it's all ready, and his room is all decorated." She began crying. "I guess he'll never use the crib…"

The parents sat with Jason in the family care room. They were now again able to see his features, which tubes and tape had previously obscured. They took pictures of him to remember him by. The nurses took prints of his feet and snipped a lock of his hair. Because the parents had been prepared for him to die and had grieved for weeks already, their sorrow now was less intense, more quiet and dignified. So when the undertaker came to get Jason, they were ready.

Though I felt relieved at his death, the ache stayed with me for a long time. Fortunately I would never again see such a tragic outcome in an infant of a diabetic mother, because with time, care of diabetic mothers improved to the point where most of their babies had normal outcomes.

13. The Grand Jury

Child abuse is a serious concern for the United States. A UNICEF report from 2007 on child wellbeing states that the United States and the United Kingdom ranked lowest among industrial nations with respect to the wellbeing of children. The introduction to this report emphasizes the following credo:

"The true measure of a nation's standing is how well it attends to its children—their health and safety, their material security, their education and socialization, and their sense of being loved, valued, and included in the families and societies into which they are born."

That the wellbeing of children is ranked low in the United States comes as no surprise. Our country does not have enough protective child legislation and does not have enough resources to prosecute crimes against children. As long as we do not have the political will to live up to the above credo, we will continue to be ranked shamefully low as regards the wellbeing of our offspring.

Among the many factors responsible for the prevalence of child abuse is the fact that 30 percent of abused or neglected children will later abuse their own children, especially if there are certain stressors in the family. Pediatricians deal with this on a regular basis, but neonatologists only rarely. The large majority of babies in our NICU were admitted directly from the delivery rooms, but a baby would at times be admitted from the outside if her gestational age (age since conception) was less than 43 weeks.

The following children were sent to us because they had been premature. They were six-week-old twins referred from an outlying hospital. The smaller twin had been hospitalized there a day earlier when the mother noticed he was lethargic and not eating well anymore. The physician had done a spinal tap, suspecting meningitis. The tap was consistently bloody, suggesting an intracranial bleed. Because of this finding he decided to refer the baby. As he was concerned about the larger twin as well, he referred both. The story was that they had been born at 35 weeks at the outlying hospital, had adequate weights and no neonatal problems, fed well and gained appropriately. One twin, however, was clearly small-for-dates, scrawny with high muscle tone, irritable, and had little self-calming behavior. After two weeks, when the smaller baby weighed five pounds, the infants were sent home from the hospital.

After the twins were admitted to the NICU, my examination showed something obviously neurologically wrong with the smaller baby. A CT scan was done which showed blood in the brain tissue and in the fluid-filled spaces of the brain. The spinal tap had not suggested meningitis. We did a CT scan on the larger twin as well, and despite no obvious neurologic or clinical signs this baby also had blood, although much less, in the brain. Small, premature babies can develop spontaneous intracranial bleeding as their vessels, poorly supported by immature brain tissue, easily rupture when increased intravascular pressure occurs; as, for example, when a baby is on a ventilator. But in these twins, born at 35 weeks and well until recently, the bleeds were not due to immaturity of their brains. The only explanation for blood in the brain was trauma.

The social worker and I sat down in my office to talk with the young father. We wanted to understand what had happened to the twins and we asked him to tell us their story from the time of their birth until they were admitted to our unit. The father was pleasant, but quiet, and answered in short sentences. This appeared to be his nature and we did not sense that he was trying to evade our questions. The mother joined us. She was very young and she talked more, but she expressed herself in trivial terms, her words almost meaningless. We got the sense that this pregnancy, the delivery of the twins, and caring for them at home, had overwhelmed them and sucked the life out of them.

As we sat talking to them, the parents related that they lived together in a trailer home. According to the mother the babies had done well for the first two to three weeks they had been home, breastfed well, the feeding supplemented with a bottle. The smallest was a voracious eater—and when admitted to our unit he almost equaled the older twin in weight— but he cried often and was difficult to soothe. About a week before, the mother said, she had noticed that the littlest was less interested in eating, slept much, and appeared lethargic when awake. The larger twin was well, she thought. She was not concerned about him.

The parents denied that the babies had ever fallen off a couch, a bed, or a changing table. They emphasized again that the crying, especially of the smaller baby, bothered them, but explained they usually picked up the babies to soothe them when this happened or let them cry themselves to sleep. We continued to probe:

"Do you ever become upset to the point of shaking the baby?"

"No, not really…Well, maybe… we could have shaken them a little bit, more like rocking," the mother said.

"Do you ever get so angry about the crying that you just can't tolerate it anymore?"

"Well, sometimes it is really hard." She was crying now. "They keep us awake so much." She looked anxiously at the father. The social worker handed her a Kleenex.

"Do you ever hit the babies?"

They appeared to ponder this question; not looking up, they just shook their heads, "No…we never hit the babies."

Yet only violent shaking of a baby or direct trauma to the head could have produced this bleeding. Maybe the parents had no sense of how violently they handled the babies, or they were in denial about it. They obviously had little experience with newborns and they could have grown up in an environment where beating young misbehaving children—even babies—was the norm. They themselves could have been abused as children.

As it turned out, further examination revealed fractures of the extremities in both children. We explained this to the parents, but they again stated they never hit the infants and they didn't know how the fractures could possibly have come about. They never became defensive. They just seemed weary that we would continue to ask them about their actions.

I felt sorry for them. They became bewildered and frightened as this nightmare unfolded. A small-for-dates infant can be a sore trial if parents are not instructed in how to deal with the baby. Swaddling helps calm him and there are many other techniques a neonatal physical therapist can teach parents to employ to calm a baby. With small-for-dates infants the most important thing is to let the parents know to call for help before they reach the point where they can't cope anymore. Neonatal units have the resources to prepare parents for taking home that kind of infant; smaller hospitals often do not.

The babies stayed in the NICU until they were well enough to be discharged to a foster home. They were feeding well, were less irritable, probably because they were hurting less as their bones healed. The littlest still exhibited neurological problems. There would eventually be a grand jury hearing to determine if the babies would be allowed to return home.

Several months later a number of us from the NICU, nurses, the social worker, the chaplain, and I—anyone who had had contact with the parents during the twins' hospital stay—were summoned to testify at the grand jury hearing in the parents' hometown ninety miles away.

Early in the morning, the day of the hearing, we arrived at the courthouse. It took a while before things got underway and the depositions lasted longer than expected. As I came before the grand jury, I noticed that the parents did not look at me. They looked detached, tired—or maybe bored—from following the proceedings. I didn't know what they were thinking. Possibly they might have asked themselves, "How could we have ended up in this situation? Has everyone in the world deserted us?" As I gave my testimony I focused on the facts, which could incriminate anyone who had cared for the infants. Members of the jury asked many questions, making this a long and involved process. As I was not present at the testimony of others who had been subpoenaed, I don't know what other evidence was presented.

The day dragged on with a lot of waiting, as the jury didn't know if they needed to hear any of us again after having heard all the testimony. I was flying to Palm Springs for a meeting that afternoon with my daughter and kept worrying that I might not make my flight.

Finally I went before the grand jury once more. By this time one of the policemen present at the hearing had volunteered to fly me to Minneapolis in his two-seater, one-engine plane to catch my flight. The small plane flight should have been enjoyable, but all I felt was the time crunch and I gave little thought to what was happening to the parents and what the verdict might be. On my way to Palm Springs I mulled over their situation, but could only speculate on what would become their and their children's fate.

The parents were convicted of abusing their children. I don't know if they got a sentence or whether the removal of the children was thought to be sentence enough. But I do know that the twins went into a foster home where they were loved and where the family eventually adopted them. Thus things turned out for the best for them. The father left the area. How the mother fared, I don't know.

14. Parental Love

I had just crashed on the sofa bed in my office at the hospital. As so often before, it had been a strenuous day, running to deliveries and C-sections, and admitting babies in distress. It was the Wednesday before Thanksgiving and thousands of snowflakes came tumbling down outside, their density obscuring visibility. Soon all was submerged under a silent white duvet. Snowmobiles rushed emergency cases and women in labor to the hospital. Some physicians skied in from home. A few night shift nurses made it to work on snowmobiles, but most failed to arrive and evening shift nurses prolonged their duties into the night.

When the phone rang I was in a deep sleep.

"I have a doctor from Ashland on the line," the operator said. "Can I patch him through?"

A silent groan escaped me and my voice was groggy, but my mind was instantly alert. Inevitably it would be about the transfer of a baby—today of all days when the world was buried in snow. The doctor came on the line. He had just delivered a two-pound-eight-ounce baby whose mother had gone into preterm labor at a neighboring small rural hospital. The physician there had sent the mother off to Duluth in an ambulance trailing a snowplow, but some 40 miles later—seventy miles from Duluth—delivery was imminent. The ambulance had stopped at Ashland Hospital. The physician in Ashland was aware that I could not rescue the baby anytime soon, but he could at least consult me, he said. The baby was beginning to exhibit signs of respiratory distress and it was evident she would soon need a ventilator. Considering that the baby had a good chance of survival, I told him to hang in there until we could get there. I confirmed that the weather in Duluth had shut everything down and talked to him about the baby's need for heat, fluids, glucose, and oxygen, and how he could best go about administering these.

I lay back in bed, trying to regain the realm of sleep, but worry kept me awake: worry for the tiny infant—not too far away—that I couldn't get to. Under normal circumstances she would have been under our care in the hour it took our transport team—sirens blaring and lights flashing—to drive to Ashland.

The physician called me frequently throughout the night about the baby's condition. He had been forced to provide care he did not feel comfortable providing and needed advice. He might have wished he could have been at home in bed sleeping, but here he was, spending the night before Thanksgiving watching over this baby. There was little he could do about the forces of nature, but he could help this infant. He had periodic blood gases drawn and reported them to me. I continued to support him with advice. His hospital had no respirators for newborns, yet as time wore on it became evident the infant could no longer breathe on her own; she was tiring. The hours and minutes of the night ticked by and morning could come none too soon.

At seven o'clock in the morning, the highway department declared the roads passable. A new nursing crew had arrived, and the worn-out evening/night shift retreated. The incubator, mounted on a stretcher, stood heated and ready, the monitors and the tackle box with equipment lined up next to it. Terry was the nurse who would be going with me. She and I quickly put on our winter gear: boots, hats, mittens, and warm coats. In the winters of northern Minnesota you want to be prepared in case of mishaps. We checked off the equipment in the ambulance before we left—oxygen, suction, appropriate connectors, etc. Hoping to get some sleep—the day would be long—I stretched out on the couch in the back.

Progress was slow. The plow had cleared a path, yet the normally one-hour drive took us two hours. Cars in the ditches along the way reminded us that the storm had just abated. On arrival at the hospital we made our way through the emergency room, down a long hallway to the nursery where we found the baby we had come for. She was lying intubated on an open bed with overhead heat. Using an ambu-bag, the exhausted physician delivered oxygen-enriched air into her lungs.

"She looks much better than she did a few hours ago," he said, yet we could tell she was in bad shape. With her tiny legs splayed open in an O, her arms extended at her sides, her translucent skin a pale pink, she was quiet and made no attempt to breathe. The physician was happy to turn her over to us. Terry and I worked for about forty-five minutes, checking x-rays, making sure the endotracheal tube was in good position. There is little leeway in the placement of the endotracheal tube in tiny babies. The physician had also placed an umbilical artery catheter. It was appropriately sutured in place and the x-rays showed it in the right position.

While Terry and I stabilized the baby, the mother tiptoed into the room. She had visited the nursery several times during the night. She seemed young and moved with a youthful grace, yet this was her ninth pregnancy. We talked about the baby, whom she and her husband had named Grace. The physician had given her information, she had understood it all, and she had a rock solid faith. Whatever God wanted for her child she would accept, she said.

The baby was a little cold. To help her retain her body heat, we greased her in Vaseline and wrapped her in flannel bandages like a mummy. There was a wonderful give and take between Terry and me, of the kind that makes teamwork a joy. We placed her in the transport incubator. I ventilated her as Terry packed up. The mom was on the other side of the incubator. Putting her hands through the portholes, she caressed Grace's forehead. The baby grasped her little finger. The mother's tiny whispered words fluttered across the open porthole. As she heard her mother's voice, Grace appeared to relax and gradually let go of her finger. We said goodbye to the mother and headed for Duluth.

Late in the day, after we had stabilized Grace in the unit, and after I had written her history, physical, and orders, I headed home for a Thanksgiving dinner prepared by Hans. He was good at this stuff: at making our home a welcoming place where family, friends, and food were valued. He had learned this at his mother's side. Fie, my mother-in-law, was an amazing woman, a good cook, and a generous hostess. Christine would later talk about holidays interrupted because of my work. On this day I was just glad to be able to be home with the family, to have a few hours to relax with my husband, my children, and my friends. Kitte and Sven Hubner and their daughters joined us. We were thankful to have them be part of our family.

Grace improved over the next several days and she was quickly weaned from the respirator. She tolerated feedings and over the next couple of weeks she put on weight. The mother came to stay in one of our family rooms as soon as the storm abated and once she had arranged care for her other children. For hours on end she sat with Grace in her arms. She pumped her breasts for nourishing milk that was fed to the baby by feeding tube. As Grace improved, the mother spent more time at home and came back on weekends, bringing her frozen breast milk.

Then one day we found that Grace's head circumference was deviating from the normal growth curve, and that the sutures—the spaces between the bones in her head—were further apart than previously. Her head size was increasing. We did an ultrasound and then did something I had never done before. Rod held a flashlight against the baby's head in a dark room to see if there were signs of hydrocephalus. What we saw completely startled us. Grace had no brain. "No brain—how could that be?" She had appeared normal, with normal movements, normal breathing, and normal reflexes. Then we reminded ourselves that all that is needed to survive at this stage of development is a brainstem. The ultrasound confirmed the diagnosis.

I looked at this normal-appearing, growing baby and thought about her humanness. As long as I had been unaware there was nothing behind the skull bones, I had considered her a human being. Now I was not so sure. To be considered a human, surely a brain must be the one essential requisite. I became aware that my feelings about Grace were changing. I had looked at her as a baby with a future, a child who would grow up in a loving family and give her parents joys and sorrows. Now she was a nothing—an empty vessel.

Meanwhile I went through the wrenching task of telling the parents. From the very beginning of the unit, we had chosen to have all support people present when discussing a baby's progress. The group usually included the neonatologist, the primary care nurse, the social worker, and the chaplain. My job was to deliver the bad news. I went right to the heart of the issue, no point in beating around the bush, no point in dwelling on the positives, about the baby feeding well and growing well. In this context, those facts were irrelevant. How could they mitigate the terrible news I had to tell the parents? They, understandably, were devastated. I showed them the ultrasound, I told them about the level at which a baby functions at this stage of development, and about how she could have seemed so normal. Terry and the social worker joined in, as did the chaplain. We had all interacted with the family and would continue to do so in the future, but we all needed to be on the same page now that our knowledge about Grace's condition had changed. It was a comfort to me—and to the family—to have those caring, sensitive people working with us. The parents never asked the question I had asked myself, "Was Grace a human being?" Despite their loss, they accepted what was happening. They had lost the child they thought Grace would become and they grieved that loss, yet even in their immense grief they continued to love and care for her until her death some months later. She was still theirs—she was Grace.

Parental love is amazing.

15. On the Helicopter

In 1989, St. Mary's Medical Center established its own helicopter service to transport accident victims from anywhere in our region and critically ill patients from referring hospitals to our hospital. The neonatal transport service would now be by helicopter, weather permitting. This mode of transport made life easier for us the neonatologists, and though at first I was uneasy about flying in the helicopter, I came to love it. I had this change of heart as soon as I had my first ride. Always, flying with both pilot and copilot made me feel safe.

Partly, my love of flying in the helicopter was due to my life-long love of adventure. This wanderlust and love of adventure was in my genes. My father was a missionary and a man of lofty ideals. Though evangelization was his passion and call, he also treasured the adventures this life provided him. He told us many stories of hunting lions in Ethiopia, of wild experiences on horseback, of finding himself in life-threatening situations because of weather and terrain. As he grew older, the stories multiplied. For me, as a neonatologist, life was also filled with high ideals and adventure. The ideals encompassed, first of all, the desire to do everything I could to heal my patient. Flying out on the helicopter to bring in sick babies belonged in the category of adventure.

When traveling by ambulance, the trips were often long and dreary and could take up to eight hours out of one's day—or night—when the rural hospital was in the far reaches of our referral area, which stretched from International Falls in Minnesota, to Hayward, Wisconsin and Ironwood, Michigan. I read, talked, or slept on the way there, worked hard to stabilize the patient at the hospital, and had to be alert to any changes in the baby on the return trip. On rare occasions, road trips were interrupted: once by a flat tire, another time by a collision with a deer.

In the first instance, Harry, an incorrigible older driver who always drove too fast, contemplated continuing on the deflated tire, but the dispatcher quickly disabused him of that notion and made us wait patiently on the shoulder of Highway Two in northern Wisconsin until another ambulance could meet up with us and bring us back. We felt fortunate to be able to provide adequate care for the baby during our wait. The incident with the deer did not inflict enough damage to hinder our progress.

One of my early trips by helicopter took me to International Falls. A three-hour trip by ambulance going out was now reduced to one hour. The call came in on a beautiful July evening.

Fred, my nurse that day, and I donned our fire-resistant flight suits and headed over to the helipad with the incubator and a large tackle box filled with our equipment. I asked Fred if he had made sure the box had been restocked since our last trip just a few hours before. Fred gave me a look that said, "Who do you think I am? Of course the box has been re-stocked," but he said nothing. He merely smiled. Fred is a man of few words. I fancied that Fred relished going to pick up babies with me. The staff at the outlying hospitals usually assumed that he was the doctor and I the nurse. As neither of us did anything to dispel this notion, I thought he might have basked in his presumed role, but he never confirmed this.

I remembered Fred from when I first came to Duluth in 1973 and was asked to give a talk on congenital heart disease to nursing students at The College of St. Scholastica. Before my talk the instructor, a nun, said to me, "We have a couple of guys in the class. They seem to understand complicated things like the heart much better than the women."

Fred was one of the guys the nun was talking about. After returning from Vietnam he had gone to college on the GI Bill. After graduation he came to work for us in the NICU. I was the only full-time female physician at the Duluth Clinic where not everyone on the all-male staff had met me with open arms, and the nun's sexist statement did not sit well with me. Fred, however, I would learn, never displayed sentiments of sexism.

On the flight deck we loaded the incubator into the back of the helicopter. Fred and I crawled in the side door and squeezed onto the bench opposite the incubator. Putting on our earmuffs with headphones so we could talk to the pilots over the engine noise, we buckled ourselves in with straps across each shoulder and around our waists.

"All set?" the chief pilot asked.

"Yup! We're all set," Fred answered.

The pilot started up the engine, soon the blades whirred, and gingerly we lifted off from the helipad.

It had been a hot day, yet we chose to leave the air-conditioner off. There was a light wind and we opened the windows of the helicopter to let in the balmy evening air. Low air pressure was of no concern as we flew at about 5,000 feet, at most. As we headed north, the sun set. Out the window I watched houses get smaller as we crested the Central Hillside, and behind me through the tail end window I saw a huge glowing full moon rise out of Lake Superior, casting its reflection on the calm mirror of the lake. We cruised north at about 150 miles per hour, across Fish Lake and Highway Four where toy cars snaked along. North of the city of Virginia, there were few houses in the landscape, and the pilot mused about how pitch dark it could be between Virginia and International Falls, but this evening the moon cast its bright light on the forests below.

We landed in International Falls, right between the hospital and the Rainy River, which here forms the border to Canada. Had we come an hour earlier, we would have seen the sun set in the river, always a spectacular sight. The pilot told us he would do a "hot unloading," meaning he was not going to shut down the engines as he wanted to go refuel at the International Falls Airport. Fred and the copilot unloaded the incubator, our monitors and tackle box, and Fred and I ducked under the blades as we pushed the incubator to the Emergency Room door. A nurse stood ready to take us upstairs to the nursery.

We took off our flight suits and put on gowns. The baby was 30 weeks gestation and weighed about three pounds. We were happy that he was not extremely small and premature, although survival rates for babies as low as 26 weeks and weighing more than one pound twelve ounces were pretty good—in the 80 percent range—at that particular time in our unit's history. The baby was lying in an incubator with an oxygen mask placed close to his face. He was struggling for air. Fred and I worked as a team. He got the endotracheal tube out of the tackle box, passed it to me, and started tearing tape. I placed a stylette through the endotracheal tube and curved the tube with the help of the stylette. Fred handed me a laryngoscope. With my hands passed through the portholes and without opening the isolette, I positioned the baby and intubated him. I took the ambu-bag that Fred had already placed in the incubator and started ventilating the baby. Fred put his hands in through the opposite portholes and taped down the endotracheal tube. He then hooked the baby up to the monitors. Fred and I traded places and he ventilated as I placed an IV. I loved this give and take of all of our nurses.

"What rate do you want?" he asked, with the IV fluids ready to go.

"About five cc per hour."

I drew blood for blood-gases from a tiny artery in the baby's wrist. The lab technician stood ready at the door to take the sample to the lab to run the gases. All this while, Fred and I had been trading back and forth, and I now ventilated the baby as Fred cleaned up the place and closed up the toolbox.

When we were finished, we shed our gowns and took turns putting on our flight suits.

We asked the nurse to take us to the mother's room. It was difficult to maneuver the incubator into the room so that Mom could see the baby face to face. This was her first baby. Tears brimmed in her eyes and she glanced tentatively toward the incubator, as if she dared not see what we had done to her baby. I told her how he was doing, why he had respiratory distress, and what to expect. Fred explained the purpose of the ET-tube and the IV. We encouraged her to put her hands through the portholes and touch the baby. As she did this, the tears rolled down her cheeks. She touched him gingerly, as if afraid to hurt him. Fred told her about the Newborn Intensive Care Unit in Duluth, told her we would call her as soon as the baby was situated in the unit, and that we would continue to keep her posted about his progress. She reluctantly withdrew her arms from the incubator, "Take good care of him," she whispered. She had delivered the baby just a few hours before and already she had to say goodbye. Fred squeezed the mother's shoulders.

"He'll be OK," he said, and he would be. Fred told Mom how to get to St. Mary's Medical Center when she was discharged the next day.

Catching up with us as we went through the emergency room, the lab technician handed us the result of the blood-gases.

A short while later we were encased in the shell of the helicopter. Fred was leaning over the incubator ventilating the baby. Outside, the moon hovered pale and luminous in the sky. The pilot started the engines. We took off, leaving the lights of International Falls behind. All we saw below was the eerie, silvery darkness of the north woods.

South of Virginia, the pilot relayed to Duluth his position and how many gallons were in the main, adding, as always, "and we have five souls onboard" (pilot, copilot, Fred, baby and me). I loved him calling us souls. Were the patient to have died would he have said "…and a corpse?" I realized I didn't know. As we came over the hill and dipped into Duluth, we saw the expanse of lights covering Park Point, stretching out towards the city of Superior. The lake remained calm. The helicopter shuddered as we set down on the helipad.

We unloaded the incubator out the back and made our way to the NICU where the nurses and the respiratory therapist stood ready to receive the baby. They put him in an isolette and connected the ET-tube to the respirator while Fred and I finished our charting and I wrote orders.

Another task accomplished. Another soul brought safely to the NICU.

16. The Father

Flying out on the helicopter to bring in sick babies was not necessarily a light-hearted adventure, as those trips sometimes became extremely stressful. The many helicopter trips I made now seem to run together in my mind, yet some stand out either because of the patient, the special circumstances, or the weather. The following story had elements of all three.

The day began innocently enough. Quietly Soo Young and I made rounds, seeing patients; recording their progress; and writing orders for cares, lab work, and medications. As the sun shone through the now grimy east windows, the usual companionable bantering between physicians and nurses took place. Though no impending high-risk deliveries threatened the day, things could change with a moment's notice. The phone rang frequently with lab results, inquiries from physicians, and mothers asking about their babies. Jewel, the unit secretary, as always, answered the phone.

Some time into the morning she handed me the phone, "A nurse from Spooner."

An urgent voice on the phone said, "We have a victim of a traffic accident: a pregnant mother who just delivered an eight-month's pregnancy." I asked her about the situation.

"That's all the information I have. I'm from another floor," she said. "The ER is in chaos, everyone is busy. Can you come get the baby?"

As we prepared for our departure, I got a call from the dispatcher who wanted to know what I weighed and asked the nurse the same. I was conscious of my weight then and always hated having to disclose it. Total weight is always a concern on flights, and particularly on that day, a dark stormy fall morning.

We were always ready to leave at a minute's notice. Debbie, the nurse who was going with me, checked the tackle box with supplies and equipment to make sure that someone had signed off that it had been restocked since it was last used. The transport incubator had been charging between transports. I thought Debbie lingered too long and my impatience showed, "Are you ready?"

"Yeah, yeah…I'm coming," Debbie said, always conscientious. "I thought I'd better put in some more five-cc syringes."

The helicopter pad was on top of the support services building a few minutes away across the skywalk. The pilots—ever ready—had already started up the helicopter. The transport incubator was loaded through the rear door, as was the tackle box. Debbie and I strapped ourselves in. Our takeoff was perilous; the helicopter swerved as soon as we left the ground, barely clearing the roof of the building next to the helipad.

Duluth is on the westernmost point of Lake Superior and as we headed across Park Point, the sandy strip that connects Duluth and Superior, Wisconsin, we received the full impact of the northeasterly wind off the lake; the helicopter swung from side to side.

By now I had been sailing on Lake Superior for years. That big body of water can be treacherous as storms often come up very fast, barely allowing time to take down the sails. The shortness of the interval between waves on that huge inland body of water makes for choppy sailing. When out in heavy weather, my usual remedy to keep seasickness at bay was to take the helm. This worked partly because it took my mind off the topsy-turvy motion of the boat, partly because it forced my eyes to focus on the horizon. This was effective on a boat. I wondered if my sailor remedies would work in the air. But taking the helm in the helicopter was of course not an option, and fixing my eyes on the horizon was nearly impossible the way the helicopter rolled. Instead the pilots turned off the heat and I closed my eyes, trying to stay detached from the rolling motion. With my crash helmet weighing heavily on my head I dozed off, and through the earphones, as if from afar, I heard the sporadic conversation between the pilots.

The north woods in all their glorious magnificence—in hues of yellow, orange and red—spread out below us, but I caught only glimpses of them when the helicopter was tipped on its side.

Sixty miles from Duluth we came in over the town where, with the helicopter hovering over the hospital, I again caught the pilot and copilot's conversation, "This is about the worst place to have a helipad!"

"See that high-power station there? The helipad is right next to it."

"Watch out on your right. Do you see those high-power wires there? Be sure you stay clear of them."

"Yeah, there are some on the other side too!"

"Boy, this wind is really throwing us around."

Both Debbie and I were worried. The ground was fifty feet away. Were the blades to catch the power lines, the helicopter could turn into a fireball. Slowly the pilots lowered us onto the pad, and finally the runners touched the ground. I relaxed.

We unloaded the incubator and our equipment. It was raining, and Debbie and I made a dash for the emergency entrance with the incubator.

Because of the overwhelming situation in the emergency room, we received only minimal preliminary information from one of the physicians. Mom had been in critical condition after the accident, her vital signs flagging. The baby had still had heart tones when the mother had arrived at the ER; the doctors had not even taken her to surgery but had quickly opened her belly right there to get the baby out. They hoped to save at least one life. By the time we arrived the mother had already been transferred to our hospital. I got a quick run-down from another physician about the newborn. The baby was forty-five minutes old. Though he had had no heartbeat at birth, a long resuscitation had stimulated the heart, which was now beating well, but he had no spontaneous movement or respiratory effort. He was being ventilated.

Just one look at the baby told me that he was dead. I thought to myself, "Why hadn't they stopped the resuscitation earlier?" If there is no response after twenty minutes there is no point in continuing. I saw no need to take the baby to the NICU. I wanted to stop the ventilation. But there was an overriding reason to transfer: the mom had been transferred. I didn't know where the father was, and for his sake, it made sense that mother and baby were in the same hospital. The baby was intubated, and ventilation gave good breath sounds on both sides. An umbilical venous catheter had been placed by one of the physicians.

As we returned to the helicopter, the pilot approached me. He was visibly upset, I noticed, and I worried about our return. We had at times aborted flights because of bad weather.

"Are there problems with our return flight?" I asked.

"No," he said. "I just want to talk to you. You have had flight instructions, haven't you?" Puzzled, I answered that indeed I had.

"Then, why did you leave the helicopter without checking with me first?" he said. It dawned on me that I hadn't. This was inexcusable and I was embarrassed. "The blades were flopping all over the place because of the wind. They could have hit you in the head."

"I ducked," I said defensively.

"Yes, but that might not have been enough. I was waiting for the blades to become more stable, and you didn't wait for my signal."

How could I have forgotten? Chastened, I assured him I would remember to do that in the future. I understood why the pilot was furious. I had put myself, and thereby the whole mission, at significant risk.

It is rare that a physician is rebuked or confronted with fury directly from a co-worker, or at least that was true in my experience. Displeasure from colleagues regarding minutiae of handling a patient, yes; fury, no. I was rather shocked by the anger of the pilot but realized I had no defense, and though I wondered to myself if the pilot would have been as high-handed with Rod, I accepted his criticism. We certainly had not needed any more catastrophes on this trip. He had in essence told me I could have had my head chopped off and that he had enough to worry about without a dumb doctor doing stupid things!

Debbie and I talked little on our return trip. The mission had been fraught with danger, but also seemed to have been without purpose. We could do nothing for the child. All that sustained the baby now was the ventilation. It was a matter of biding time until the father could be located.

When back at St. Mary's, I called to the ICU where the mother was taken. She had been declared dead shortly after arrival. They hadn't heard from the father yet; they would tell him to call the NICU as soon as he contacted them.

I felt unable to concentrate on anything, but forced myself to finish my rounds. My thoughts were with that father. Circumstance had thrown me into a relationship with this person I didn't know and toward whom I had a duty: to tell him of the imminent death of his child. I didn't know with what information the police had gone to find him. I didn't know what hopes he might have for his child. Only a few hours before, with no cloud on the horizon—at least that is how I liked to imagine it—this man had had a healthy young wife who was expecting their first child. I sympathized with the first ones to have contact with the father—the police: how horrendously difficult it was being the bearers of bad news, especially if the news was unanticipated. As for me, talking to this father was a job I gladly would have given to anyone else.

When he called his voice was barely audible.

"How is my son?"

Playing for time, I said, "The baby is on a respirator." I hesitated to tell him much more. First I needed to know something about this man. What did he already know? I knew nothing about the nature of the accident. Did he know the particulars? Did he know his wife was dead?

"Have you talked to the ICU here?"

"Yes," he said.

"What did they tell you?"

"My wife is dead," he said, and then…nothing. The voice, disembodied and monotonous, floated away, filled with a grief he could not yet comprehend. I choked up.

"How is the baby?" he asked again.

"The baby is critical," I said—now ready to elaborate more. I told him the baby was on a respirator, wasn't breathing on his own. Though the heart was beating, we did not expect him to survive.

Why didn't I tell him outright that the baby was, in fact, already dead? By my words I was implying the baby was dying, yet I refrained from telling him the baby was dead. Why? I suppose I wanted him to have hope, for just a little while. I wanted him to see the baby. I wanted him to be here with his child, holding the baby when we took him off life support. Maybe it was cruel of me not to tell him, but he had just heard that his wife had died. How could I tell him that his baby son too was dead? I didn't know the father and didn't know what was best for him. I repeated what we were doing for the baby, and asked him where he was. He said he was at home in Wisconsin. Family was with him. He would leave shortly.

"Can you have someone bring you?" I asked. "I don't think you should be driving."

"I'll be OK." His voice was devoid of emotion, and utterly bereft...

I don't know if he came alone or if someone brought him. He called from the ICU where he had just seen his wife's body. He was crying now. I related to him the baby's entire course from the time of birth and told him we needed to take him off life support. If he would like, we would wait till he came to the NICU.

"No," he said, "I don't want to see the baby. Just take him off life support now."

I tried to tell him that he might be grateful later that he had seen the baby, but he was so besieged with grief for his wife that he had nothing left with which to grieve for the baby. He may have wanted to deny the reality of his child. Did he fear that if he saw him he would be forced to acknowledge him as a person, as his son? Did he fear the terrible emotions that would bring to his already beleaguered soul?

He never came to the NICU.

We took the baby off life support, took several pictures of him, took his footprints, and cut off a lock of his hair, thus collecting a few mementos of his brief life to give to the father who never got to hold him. We did this in the hope that someday he would want to know what his son had looked like, in the hope that one day he would have the energy to grieve for him.

17. Having It All?

It was a beautiful day at the cabin, one of those hot summer days of 2012 when only the lake gave solace; its waters shimmered in the sun. We were cleaning up the beach after a heavy storm that had downed branches and lifted a panel right off the dock, depositing it in the lake, never to be found. Grandchildren were in and out of the water, on the speedboat, and trying out the wake skis for the first time. Hans and I had walked out to the point that belongs to our property to look at the beaver lodge. The busy beaver had taken down more trees since we had last been there.

We came back and joined our adult children who were talking, reading, and watching the grandkids. Christine was talking about an article she had read in *The Atlantic* by Anne-Marie Slaughter: *Why Women Still Can't Have it All*. I was listening desultorily, and midway into the discussion I said blithely, "Well, I had it all, and I was fine." My working life was sixteen years in the past, and it was even longer since I had been a working mother. The distance of time had shed a rosy hue on that era. I had taken care of my children, my family, *and* my work, and I had managed just fine. Yes, I had had it all.

Christine, now forty-three, turned to me and said, "But it wasn't that easy, Mom. I remember times when I felt alone and abandoned, especially in my junior high years, and I know it wasn't easy for you either. You were often tired, depressed and had no energy. You always needed to sleep." She said it without acrimony. She just wanted to set the record straight. As she said these words I felt a pang, the pang of pain I had experienced throughout my career as I was torn between conflicting loyalties, between being available to my family and being there for my patients.

I thought back to how hard I had worked. For the first four years there were only two neonatologists, Rod and me. Though we occasionally had backup from the pediatricians, we basically alternated calls. When Soo Young joined us, we changed the call schedule so we continued to work for two weeks being on call every other day, but now with one week off in between. It lightened the load, but even then, taking into consideration the week we didn't work and including calls, we averaged seventy hours per week. I was never able to sleep during the daytime, so it seemed I was always trying to catch up on sleep but never did.

This work schedule was hectic and worked only as long as there were no unanticipated events. I felt blessed that my children were healthy and rarely sick. Had I had a sickly child or one with a chronic disease I could not have done it. I remember when Christine had the chickenpox. I think she came down with the pox on a Friday, but Monday morning she was feeling sicker than ever and I was in a dilemma. I was on call, and since Soo Young, having been on call for the weekend, had already worked for seventy-two hours straight and Rod, with the week off, was out of town, there was no way I couldn't go to work. It was not just the patients that were at issue. I had to take my colleagues into consideration. We had such a small department; there were only the three of us, and we all worked equally hard, so I didn't want to put an extra burden on my colleagues if I could help it.

Meanwhile our kind neighbor had said that Christine could come to her house and she would take care of her. Though I was grateful, I felt bad about taking her up on this. I knew Christine would be well cared for, but she needed her mother. I remember being sick as a child and my mother doting on me. That's what you long for, even as an adult, when you are sick. I knew I should be with my daughter.

The issue of working moms has been much in the news lately. *The New York Times Magazine* one Sunday had a photo-essay of the "other mothers" of Manhattan: the nannies who care for many high-powered women's children. Those children are fortunate to have at least one steady person, other than their parents, who loves them and cares for them. But what about the women who cannot afford that kind of care, who are forced to work because the family needs the income, or the single mothers who must work to support themselves and their children?

Our family did not need my income. We could have managed comfortably without it. However, I had invested years in my education, and I had done it while being a mom, knowing that this would be an enterprise between my family and my work. It had been easier for me in Denmark when the children were young, because of the excellent childcare offered. On the other hand, when you are a young parent with small children, you think it will be easier when the kids get older and are in school, yet many agree that teenagers probably need you the most. I didn't know that when my kids were little. There was a lot I didn't know and that society as such didn't know. We women who got an education and entered the workforce in the sixties and seventies had to work hard to prove ourselves, to prove that we were as smart as—and could work as hard as—the men whose jobs we were competing for; that's how it was looked at. It was uncharted territory, but we went about it sure that we could do it and be great moms as well...that we could "do it all!"

So I wasn't going to ask for special privileges from my colleagues to stay home with a sick child. That wasn't done. Women of the seventies felt that the only way to be accepted was to be like the men. The men didn't stay home with their sick kids. They had wives. Sometimes I wished I had a wife, and in a sense I did. I had a spouse who cooked and cleaned and took care of our kids. The problem was that he wasn't home all the time, either. He too had a job, and though he, because of a lesser workload, might more easily have stayed home with Christine, he didn't do that. Men just didn't stay home with sick kids, at least not then. This often preyed on my mind when there were conflicts between family and work.

When we lived in Kansas City and Rochester, we had brought first Inge, then Mette, with us from Denmark. These were women who cared for our kids when we were gone, and in Mette's case also did housework and cooked. We had asked Mette to come with us to the US again, but she had turned us down. Besides it had turned out to be impossible to get a visa for her on an indefinite basis. So after moving to Duluth, we had relied on various women and young girls to care for the house and children. This had not worked successfully until we got Rachel, a college student who worked for us for about four years.

It had been a struggle at times, and leaving our teenaged children alone so much had led to problems, especially for Michael. He had gotten into trouble—most of it innocent and certainly not something that attracted the attention of the law—though we didn't know the half of it until he confessed some of his many transgressions to us as an adult. We were naive about teenagers. Since we had both been the golden children in our families, we could not conceive of children not having the same sense of responsibility as we had.

So when on that summer day at the cabin I said I had had it all, maybe I meant that I had had the best half of each world: my family world and my working world. Working families cannot have it all until the work environment takes into consideration that people—men and women—have obligations beyond their work. Only when family and work environments dovetail can we have a harmonious integration of work and family life for all, women *and* men. It seems unlikely that this will happen soon in the U.S. I think that European countries have far more family-friendly policies, from which we could learn much if our legislators didn't have a pathological fear of the U.S. becoming a socialist country. And if their worry is about productivity, it may come as a surprise that according to a 2009 survey by the Swiss bank UBS, France, which has the shortest workweek among industrialized nations, at the time had a higher productivity than the United States.

While it would have been much easier being a woman physician in Denmark, Hans and I had agreed to let professional opportunities determine where we lived, though it wasn't an easy decision; we knew that Danish family-friendly policies would have better accommodated our needs as a family. And despite the fact that I was a very capable physician, the stigma of being a woman remained. The issue didn't present itself on a daily basis and over the years, with the addition of more women physicians at the Duluth Clinic, the climate changed somewhat.

18. Uncertainty

At three o'clock in the morning the phone rang, jolting me out of a heavy sleep. I was in my bed at home and I quickly grabbed the phone so it wouldn't wake Hans. I was used to getting calls at all hours. It was my job to get out of bed in the middle of the night for babies in distress, but I rarely welcomed the calls.

A birth is dictated by circumstances in the mother's body—that is the way it has been throughout the history of mankind—and it will continue this way, unless we allow all deliveries to be by scheduled Caesarian sections in order to inconvenience neither mother, doctor, nor nurse. In this case labor started when nature dictated and for me that night, it meant getting up at three in the morning. I was grateful that I had already had four hours of sleep, and that because it was summer it was almost light and a beautiful summer morning.

The dispatcher informed me that the neonatologist of an NICU in Wisconsin wanted our team to transport a baby from a small town to his hospital. The small town was in his NICU's service area. Since the baby was very small and in distress, he wanted it transported by air, but as his NICU, for whatever reason, had no air transport at the moment, he turned to us.

I quickly threw on the scrubs lying by my bed, scooped up my car keys, and in thirteen minutes flat I was in the NICU. Everything was ready: one of our nurses, Denise, the tackle box, and the incubator were already at the helipad. As the request from said NICU was extremely unusual, I got on the phone with the neonatologist before leaving to make sure the message was correct. It was—never doubt a dispatcher! I ran to my office, scrambled into my flight suit, and hightailed it to the helicopter. We were in the air less than half an hour after the call came in.

Still not wholly awake, I rested my back against the cabin wall and dozed off; sleep was near impossible while sitting upright on a narrow metal bench, my knees scrunched up against the incubator, a heavy helmet on my head.

In the warm summer morning we left the windows of the helicopter open. As we flew southeast into Wisconsin, the sun crept above the horizon and with the growing light we saw the landscape below: the north woods had been left behind and we were now flying over open, verdant farmland. After about forty-five minutes we were over the small town. The pilot identified the hospital on the river, and landed in a cleared parking lot.

None of our crew was familiar with this hospital. We scanned the building for an emergency entrance, unsure of where to go. Just then an orderly appeared. He led us through winding corridors, up elevators, and down hallways to one of the operating rooms. As we entered, the queasy sweet odor of amniotic fluid greeted us. The scene was chaotic! Wrappings from numerous packages of sterile equipment were on the floor and on every piece of furniture, indicating things hastily requested, found to be wrong, discarded, and new requests made. The mother had been moved from the operating table to her room, but the tiny baby was on a table under radiant heat. Their work done, several nurses, an anesthetist, and two doctors were just waiting for us to take the baby off their hands. The doctors identified themselves and told me the mother had presented in an advanced stage of labor at 26 weeks gestation; a C-section was done because the baby was a breech presentation and—despite having had her own baby only a week before—the town's only pediatrician had quickly arrived to care for the newborn.

Everything was handled well. The two-pound-nine-ounce baby boy was intubated and was being ventilated. He had been kept warm under radiant heat and was pink and spunky. The position of the endotracheal tube was appropriate. No umbilical catheter was in place; the pediatrician had attempted to place it, but had been unsuccessful. I opted for a peripheral IV to infuse dextrose to keep the baby's blood sugar up. After greasing the baby in Vaseline and wrapping him like a mummy to keep him warm, Denise gently eased him into the incubator.

A nurse from maternity led the way as we rolled the incubator with the baby down the hall so Mom could see her son. Before entering the mother's room the nurse told us Mom was mentally challenged, and the fact that she needed a C-section had been upsetting and confusing to her. We wedged the stretcher with the incubator between beds to show the baby to his mother, a dozing, small, and somewhat chubby young girl.

"Jodie," the nurse said in a raised voice, "they are here with your baby; take a look." The mother opened her eyes; disoriented she looked around and started to whimper. The anesthesia was wearing off and she was becoming aware of her pain.

"Take a good look, Jodie; you may not see him for a while." By opening up a porthole in the incubator so she could see the baby's face, Denise encouraged the mother to look at her baby and touch him. But Jodie cried out and squirmed in bed.

"Ouch! I am hurting down there," she pointed to her lower abdomen. "It's really killing me! Ouch! I want it to go away."

"I'll go get you some pain pills in a little bit. But take a look at the baby. You haven't really seen him yet," the nurse said.

Jodie did not look toward the baby. I wondered if she really knew she had been pregnant, but the nurse said she had known for some months. Right now, however, the baby seemed to be the least of her concerns.

"Jodie, the baby is very small, and he needs extra special help. He is therefore going to a newborn unit where they care for babies born too early," Denise said.

It became clear that Jodie had no idea what was going on; we simply could not get her attention.

"What happened to me? Why am I hurting so much? Ouch! Help me."

"Remember, you started having pains last night and you came to the hospital," the nurse said. "The baby was coming but he was coming feet first, so the doctor took you to surgery and cut you open down there, so he could take out the baby. That was what was best for your son." Her voice was still raised as if speaking louder would make Jodie understand better.

But Jodie thrashed and whimpered. She was immensely frightened and the pain was obviously affecting her more now. Denise talked to her, trying her best to make her understand the situation, but to no avail.

"We have to take the baby to the special unit. We are going by helicopter, so he will get there quickly. He needs to be where he can get good and very specialized care," I said. But for Jodie, only her pain was real. She was so distraught that she would understand nothing until her pain was brought under control and she was feeling better.

Outside the room, the nurse gave us some sketchy information about the father: he had been in a bar in town, she thought, when the baby was about to be delivered; it was known that he spent much of his time there. In all the chaos of quickly moving Jodie to surgery for the needed C-section, no one had thought to try to locate him until later, to tell him of the baby's arrival. He had not yet been found. For unknown reasons none of Jodie's relatives were present.

We made our way back to the helicopter.

Thirty-five minutes later we were at the hospital where the NICU was located. As we landed in a cordoned-off parking lot, employees were streaming toward the hospital for the day shift. We brought the baby to the Newborn Intensive Care Unit where nurses and the neonatologist-on-call took over. Before leaving we gave them the information we had on the baby and parents.

To have provided care for a baby that would be followed in another NICU is anticlimactic. Yet to have the baby in the closest NICU was best for the parents, especially these parents. I didn't envy the staff there; working with this marginal family would take a lot of effort. Would the mother and father bond with the baby? Would the father even be involved? Traveling the distance of fifty miles from home to the NICU might prove to be insurmountable for them; they might see little of the baby during his very long hospital stay. Would the mother keep the baby? And if she did, would she be able to learn to give adequate care? Or would the baby be abused because the mother misinterpreted his signs of hunger or pain? Would the baby end up being adopted? One could merely speculate about these questions; only as the baby grew and the staff and social workers got to know the parents and their competences, would one have an idea of what was the best course, and maybe there would never be a good solution.

All these thoughts occupied me as we headed back to Duluth to start the day's work in our own NICU.

19. Denial

Iloved doing what I sometimes thought of as "snatching patients from the arms of death and returning them to health"—the more critical the patient, the better. Nowhere are the possibilities for dramatic results greater than in pediatrics and neonatology. Children recover fast and often completely. The mundane tinkering with chronic patients to bring them into a somewhat better state of health—a tedious and sometimes unsatisfying process—was not for me. I wanted challenges every day of my working life. Being a neonatologist provided me with plenty of those.

Caring for newborns is most often gratifying. However, there are situations when you know that the family and you will be struggling for days to maintain hope, only to lose it. Parents, who have long tried to have a baby, who have already had several pregnancies with early losses, who now have made it to 25 weeks in the present pregnancy, and who finally have a live baby, are filled with a mountain of hope. But the baby is sick from the start, her lungs immature, only the respirator keeping her alive. I know that the chances the baby will survive are minimal. The parents are aware the baby only hangs on to life by a very fragile thread, yet they cling to hope. The longer the baby survives, the more hope grows. So when the baby dies, they are shattered, yet also grateful for the time they had with her. Parents have taught me much about how hope can sustain you and how, when all hope is lost, positive memories can remain.

Though the less dramatic ones were far more frequent, it is the tragic cases that have remained in my memory. They remain with me because they preyed and continue to prey on my emotions: congenital malformations of a genetic nature for which there is no cure; congenital heart problems, many of which now can be corrected, but entail significant surgeries; fetal effects of high-risk pregnancies; and unintentional abuse by ignorant parents, including maternal substance abuse.

One such case was my patient, Erik.

The helicopter took off in the rain, but barely over the hill, it turned around. Rain was turning to sleet and we could not make it to our destination. After a significant wait, the ambulance was ready and two hours later we were at the Big Fork Hospital. We found our patient, a term baby, in the nursery. We had been called when the now one-day-old baby had started having some mild respiratory distress, wasn't feeding, and had a mottled appearance. I evaluated him, got cultures, and started an IV and antibiotics.

When I asked to see the parents, the nurse told me that the mother was unmarried and was giving the baby up for adoption. She had not wanted to see him. Nonetheless, I wanted to talk to her. She should know what was going on with her child. This was her right, at least until the adoption was completed.

The mother was a twenty-year-old college student, who listened quietly to what I told her, but said little in response and had no questions. As I talked more to the nurse afterward, I learned that the mother had come home to her parents' house for Christmas. It was presumed that she knew she was pregnant but had not told her parents, who had suspected nothing; she showed little under a large sweatshirt. When she went into labor shortly before Christmas she was taken to the hospital for stomachaches and the truth was revealed to her parents. The nurse said that the young woman had no relationship with the father of the baby.

We brought the baby to Duluth, and the next morning the grandparents came. They seemed to be a caring couple, wanting to know everything about the baby whom they had seen at birth; they now named him Erik. The grandmother sat with him for a long time. She said their daughter was home and that she held firm on wanting to give Erik up for adoption. She still did not want to see him. She was preparing to go back to school as soon as the Christmas holidays were over.

It soon became apparent that Erik did not have sepsis as first suspected. Further auscultation of the heart in the NICU unmasked abnormal heart sounds. An echocardiogram revealed a congenital heart condition, hypoplastic left heart, which at that time was inoperable. I had conversations with the pediatric cardiologists in Minneapolis about the baby and sent the echocardiogram to them. They agreed that they could offer nothing. Distraught at this news, the grandmother sat by the Erik's bed for hours, crying. The grandfather remained with her when they visited and was clearly also affected by the course of events. Their daughter still did not come.

As it became clear that the baby was dying, I urged the grandparents to encourage the mother to see Erik—she should give herself a chance to get to know him before she had to say goodbye—and eventually the mother did come. She seemed to be a young woman who had always known what she wanted, who had set her course and was unwilling to deviate from it. She was pleasant and intelligent, but it was evident that she was trying very hard not to be involved and to put this whole thing behind her. I wondered, "Had it been date rape? Could she not bear to see the baby because it might remind her of the father? Or was it a boyfriend that she still loved? Or was it because she could not bear to face the one slip-up she had ever made in her life thus far?" She didn't say anything, though I suspected she was a woman who might be very articulate in a different context. She looked at Erik, she touched him, but it was as if she shrunk away from him. She would not allow herself to feel anything for this child.

I felt sadness for her. She must have been in denial throughout her pregnancy. During the delivery she must have heard the baby, even though she didn't see him. How could she feel nothing? Even our social worker could get little out of her. I hoped sincerely that she talked to her parents, though they did not reveal anything about her. It appeared they were a very tight-knit family who would not allow strangers a look inside their lives. Or were they just numb, unable to express what they felt?

We had conferences with the family, discussing Erik and the course of his disease. The grandparents asked appropriate questions, showed concern for both Erik and their daughter, who was also present, but they did not share their feelings. These people were of stoic Scandinavian stock, among whom everything is borne with an outward appearance of coping well and not needing support.

When Erik died, the family sat together in the family room taking turns holding him. The grandmother and the mother cried silently with tears streaming down their faces, uttering nothing. The mother would not let go of Erik. Hour after hour she sat there holding him—continuing to hold him throughout the night. Never had we had a mother who held her baby for that long after death.

I have often wondered how she fared in life. Was she able to go back to school, continue her studies, and get her degree? Was she able to forget, or was it a nightmare that continued to haunt her? I would never know.

20. Dave

It was a familiar scenario. A frantic call from an outlying hospital to the NICU, "We need you," and then hurried explanations that only afforded us a tiny window into what was going on. But it mattered little. The fact was that the doctors in that hospital had desperately needed us for a half hour or more, and all we could do was try to get there as fast as possible. Sometimes I wished that I had the ability to see into the future, that I had known hours before that disaster would strike this mother fifty miles away from our center. I longed to be able to create alternate scenarios because the "what ifs" haunt you. What if the mother had had symptoms that had sent her to our hospital before the incident? Or what if we had been able to keep her alive on life support until the baby was delivered?

Philip Roth, in his book *The Plot Against America*, creates a "what if" situation. His novel traces the impact on America and American Jews in a world where Charles Lindbergh, a Nazi-sympathizer, becomes president in 1940 instead of Roosevelt, with the U.S. occupied by Hitler's forces. He does an extremely plausible job of it and creates a frightening scenario. Stephen King, in his book *11/22/63*, posits the "what if" of Kennedy not being assassinated, but the alternate scenarios he dreams up are not necessarily better. It is satisfying, however, to ponder a "what if" when an alternate scenario could have changed the outcome for the better, if the alternate scenario of this story could have prevented the death of a mother and her child.

Now that I look back with the facts in hand I want to imagine the situation:

It was a warm summer day in the small town in northeastern Minnesota that we were called to. School was out and the children of the town were positively giddy about the long summer vacation that stretched before them. Little Dave, ten years old, took a long time getting home from school that day. First he made his way to the baseball diamond where he played for awhile, then he got into a fight with a neighbor kid. Now dawdling and taking his time, he eventually reached the house on the other side of town where he and his mother lived. He was an only child and now there was just the two of them, his mom and him. His stepfather had left the family a few months before, but with the baby in his mother's belly they'd soon be three again. His mom didn't work, and she never seemed to have much money, but they always had enough to eat. He was happy his stepfather had left; he was always angry, it seemed, and often beat both his mom and him. Things were better now.

As he approached the house he could see that his mother had done the laundry and hung it outside to dry. He crawled through the fence and ran across the backyard and up the steps leading to the back porch. Once inside, he inched off his backpack and got out of his shoes calling out, "Mom, I'm home!" There was no answer and the house was remarkably quiet. He wondered if she was even home, but their car, an old rusty wreck, was parked outside. Maybe she had gone to a neighbor. He would go get a snack before she got home.

He walked into the kitchen and there—lying on the floor—was his mom. He called out to her, but she didn't move. Her face was gray; her eyes looked straight ahead, not noticing him. She was making funny noises when she breathed. He lifted her arm. "Mom, what's the matter?" The arm was limp and plunked to the floor when he let it go. Though frightened, he knew this was a situation where he needed to call 911, and he ran to the phone. Someone would be here really soon, he thought. Fortunately, the dispatcher knew his last name and knew where they lived, and she said she would send an ambulance immediately.

"Is anyone with you?" she asked Dave. When he said no, she told him to go to a neighbor, but he knew he wasn't going to leave his mother. He stood with the phone in hand and looked at her, unsure of what to do next. She still had that noisy breathing. He hoped someone would come soon. He put the phone back in the cradle; then he went and lay down by his mother and put his ear to her chest; her heart was beating. He stayed there by her, holding her hand, listening for the sirens of the ambulance.

He watched the EMTs struggle to get the bulk of his mother onto a stretch-er. A woman with the ambulance team took him aside and told him she was going to bring him to his aunt; the neighbor wasn't home, she said. He resisted and began crying; he wanted to stay with his mom; if he didn't stay something bad would happen. The woman told him it would be better if he didn't go to the hospital by himself. They would be working to make his mom better and he could not be present. His aunt would take him to the hospital later to see his mother and then the doctor would have had time to figure out what was going on.

When the NICU team and I were on our way in the helicopter to the small town, I didn't have this story. I only knew that a mother had been brought into the emergency room with an apparent stroke, and that the local doctors were planning to do a C-section to save the baby. We landed in the parking lot of the small one-story rural hospital. After unloading the incubator and our equipment tool kit from the helicopter, we ran to the ER.

We walked into a large room where, as is often the case when an emergency overwhelms the capacity of a small hospital, everything was in disarray. Clearly several doctors had been called from the clinic. The mother, an American-Indian woman, had arrived in much the same state as she was in when Dave had found her. No one knew how long she had been unconscious and with compromised breathing. She was intubated, given oxygen and drugs to stimulate her heart, but didn't improve. The team of doctors was now faced with the issue of whether to continue resuscitating her or turn their attention to the baby, whose heartbeat they could still discern. About twenty minutes after the mother's arrival, they undertook the C-section. It was done right in the ER. They quickly opened up the mother's belly and got the baby out. At birth the baby—a girl—had not breathed, was limp and had the color of slate, but she still had a heartbeat.

One of the doctors was ventilating the infant when our team arrived. We took over the resuscitation. The baby was near term. She had a weak, slow heartbeat, her skin was pale without perfusion, and her nail beds and tongue dark blue; she was limp, without spontaneous movement. The doctor said that despite being well ventilated, she hadn't really changed since birth and her color had not improved. I suspected the baby was near death, but we went through the motions anyway. Though I knew with full certainty that we couldn't get her back, I wanted the team at the hospital to feel their call to us has not been in vain and that everything was being done. That's how it always is: rather do too much than too little. So after quickly giving intracardiac epi, we put in an umbilical catheter, and gave epinephrine, calcium, and bicarbonate, all the while continuing ventilation and heart compressions. Very little changed. There was only a passing change in the quality of the heartbeat and the heart rate, which quickly waned again.

While thus occupied, I told the doctors about the outlook as I saw it, and that I would not transfer the baby. They were disappointed. They had pinned their hopes on at least saving the baby, but I told them the baby was essentially dead. We had now resuscitated for close to forty-five minutes with no response. "In a baby, the heart sometimes goes on beating at a slow rate for a long time," I said. They accepted this, and five minutes later I was able to pronounce the baby dead. The heart had stopped.

This is always a heart-wrenching situation. The doctors in the referring hospital had done all they could to save the mother. She had gestational diabetes and hypertension. She had been inconsistent in following the recommended treatments. When she presented in the emergency room they had little chance of saving her, but they had hoped that maybe they could save the baby. However, the baby had probably suffered lack of oxygen for quite some time. No one knew how long the mother had lain on the floor with inadequate respiration and a weakening heart before Dave found her.

Our team was used to rescuing babies, or at least getting a significant chance at reversing the course of events. None of us liked flying out to get a baby and returning with no patient; I remember no other time it happened to me. Somehow we all, the local doctors and my crew, felt as if we had failed somewhere along the line, but in reality we had all been presented with hopeless situations, in regard to both mother and child.

The local doctors had kept the aunt abreast of what was happening, and as I was leaving I also talked to her and to Dave. All I could tell them was that there was nothing that I could have done for the baby, and that the physicians here had done everything in their power for both mother and child. None of that was enough, because the mother was close to death when Dave had found her. Dave looked at me teary-eyed, his mouth drooping, lips quivering, looking lost. I knew that the baby was not on his mind; he was just trying to comprehend the loss of his mother. I wanted to scoop him up, cradle him in my arms, and tell him everything would be okay. But I had no words to comfort either him or his aunt, and of course everything wouldn't be okay; his life was falling apart, his immediate future uncertain. He didn't realize that yet, however; all he knew was that there was hope no more, since his mom was gone. What both he and his aunt needed was for people who knew them to gather around them and lift them up. I fell short on these points: I was not part of their family or their culture.

I left the hospital with a sense of a crushing defeat and felt an enormous sadness for the family I had not been able to help.

21. Retirement

By the mid-eighties all our children had left home and I continued to work an unchanged call schedule with my two colleagues. Week followed week, month followed month, and I continued to love what I was doing. Every new patient represented a challenge, every new problem begged for a solution, and every family needed reassurance. Hans was in the prime of his career, having become an endoscopist of note. He now worked harder than ever, though his call schedule continued to be much lighter than mine, but with the kids gone we had more time for each other.

Besides our work in the unit, the neonatologists took turns working in the follow-up clinic where we saw children who had been patients in the NICU. Working there was a diversion from the hectic pace of the unit. The group of patients we saw included all preemies below a certain gestational age and all others about whom we had concerns at discharge. This free, hospital-supported clinic had been started in the late 1970's and operated two to three times per week, initially following patients to age five years, later to age three. Our support staff consisted of a co-ordinator, a social worker, a dietician, and a physical therapist. The staff was amazing and very supportive of the families that we saw. We had the opportunity to intervene where there was failure to thrive, when cerebral palsy was diagnosed in babies with birth trauma or in preemies, and when other physical and developmental problems presented. The social worker explored the home environment with the parents to make sure it was supportive of the child's needs. The dietician gave advice about appropriate diet, evaluated growth, and helped parents with children who weren't thriving, while the neonatal physical therapist evaluated development. I learned much about normal and abnormal development in children from the latter. We were continually in awe at how many of our littlest preemies were doing well and developing normally, but needless to say, there were also many with developmental problems. Survival rates for infants 24-28 weeks had risen steadily, but their numbers were too small to show any significant trend. For babies 28-32 weeks the survival rate by the early nineties was 95-100 percent, and most babies above those gestational ages survived. Outcomes had also improved. It was a joy to see these very small babies grow and thrive. After the evaluation we sent recommendations to the children's physicians.

I sometimes thought about what our situation might have been, had we stayed in Denmark. After so many years in the United States, however, and having become American citizens, we felt that our home was in the U.S. That is, until we returned to Denmark for vacations. We had kept the farmhouse that we had bought in 1966 with Hans's parents. After they died, it continued in our ownership, and when staying there we felt Danish and at home. But we agreed that we were happy that we had not pursued a career in Denmark. My friend from the *gymnasium*, Karen, with whom I had started medical school in Aarhus, brought this home to me early on. She went into private practice as a family practitioner when she finished her training. She lasted twelve years. She said that while most of her patients and families were wonderful to work with, there were among her patients some who made life miserable for her, calling her up at all hours of the day or night, often berating her in anger when she wouldn't prescribe what they wanted or didn't like a diagnosis she had given. This was a patient population that seems foreign to us here in Minnesota. Maybe this was the flip side of the welfare state. These patients had become accustomed to getting what they wanted, when they wanted it. Karen had nightmares about being confronted by angry patients, waking up sweat-drenched and losing sleep over it. So, much to my surprise—she had been a dedicated physician—she gave up medicine and retired when she was yet in her forties. Immigration to the U.S. had been the right thing for us. We were spared many frustrations and had been given the opportunity to be involved in the development of exciting new subspecialties—Hans in endoscopy and I in neonatology.

Anxiety was not what caused my own lack of sleep; rather it was caused by having too much to do of what I loved. However, I found I needed other interests to take my mind off my work. I went back to school and got a Bachelor of Music degree. I had not intended to do that, had simply started taking piano lessons to pick up where I had left off after six years of piano playing as a child. When on call, in the days before the cell phone, I needed to stick close to a phone, and unable to participate in my family's outdoor activities I found solace in the piano. One thing led to another and I ended up with a degree in piano performance. I then began a Master of Liberal Studies degree. That degree was pure luxury and fun. I could take any classes I wanted— almost—but concentrated on art and literature of the nineteenth century, ethics, and African history. While writing papers for my classes I realized how much I enjoyed this activity, and it is not surprising that writing became a major interest of mine in retirement.

Later, as I reached my middle fifties I began to realize that working intensely for two weeks, then spending a week catching up on sleep, was taking too much joy out of my life. I worked and slept, was always tired, and was not prepared to continue that way for much longer. I kept telling my colleagues that I wanted to retire, but in essence what I desperately needed was to have my sleep disrupted less. To that end I had tried having a woman neonatologist from Hibbing work for me part-time, but this was not satisfactory to me, as I felt unable to provide the continuity of care I treasured. I finally decided that since the schedule wasn't going to change, I would go.

The Duluth Clinic proposed a retirement party. Just retiring was hard enough, I thought, but celebrating it…no! So I turned it down. Besides, there were only, at most, a dozen doctors out of several hundred who had worked closely with me and could reflect meaningfully on my work and retirement, and such reflection would accentuate the finality of my decision: that I indeed would leave St. Mary's/Duluth Clinic. Then St. Mary's Hospital and the NICU nurses wanted to throw me a party; I couldn't turn that down. These people meant the world to me. Many reflected on the years we had worked together; it was a joyful celebration, and I felt very touched. Yet I also felt increasingly sad that this was it: the end of the life in medicine that I had so enjoyed.

Then, a few years after I retired, the department added nurse practitioners; with those people on board, night call was reduced. Had I only been able to hang in there a little longer, I sometimes thought, I could have continued working another five or six years. But in retrospect it proved a blessing. It placed something within my grasp that I had thought lost: the goal I had set myself as a fourteen-year-old to work—if not in Aden—then at least in another developing country.

But adjusting to retirement proved far from easy. I retired July 1, 1996. Ten days later I went on a trip to Namibia, and not until I came home did I get a taste of retirement, and didn't like it. I had just turned fifty-nine, and there seemed to be no purpose to my life any longer. I could sleep all I wanted—something I hadn't been able to do for so long—and for the rest of the time I could read, tend my garden, and bike—something I loved. Hans had not retired yet, so that left me many hours of the day alone at home. The many years of hard work hadn't afforded me many opportunities to nurture friendships, especially friendships with women; I had few close friends. None of the hobbies or other pursuits were enough to satisfy me. Like many retirees, I felt an emptiness I hadn't expected. I missed the discipline and order of getting up each morning and going off to do meaningful work. So much of my life had been tied up in being a doctor, and now I had lost that identity.

These doldrums lasted only about six months, however.

IV. Closing the Circle

22. A Journey Back in Time

Unconsciously, I must have anticipated this emptiness, since I had grasped at the opportunity to travel to the fledgling nation of Namibia on the African continent within ten days after I retired.

I traveled with a group of representatives from U.S. Lutheran colleges that had hosted Namibian students over the previous ten years, and were traveling there to visit the former students and to see how they fit into their newly independent country. I had simply tagged along with the group although my reasons for going were vague, other than an interest in visiting a developing African nation and a desire to stall my retirement.

It was an amazing trip. I learned much about that small country's struggle for independence from South Africa, obtained as late as 1990, and I met many courageous people who had participated in that struggle. More importantly for me it became a journey back in time to my childhood in Aden, and as we traveled a seed germinated in me, a seed that had lain dormant for decades.

We had left Windhoek, the capital of Namibia, at dawn some days before. On the way, the small, isolated mountains called *inselbergs* changed from dark shadow to golden pink to bright red to brown as the sun rose. Their jagged forms were so like the volcanic rocks of Aden, the city of my youth. On both sides of the road the scrub desert stretched to the horizon.

In the town of Swakopmund, on the Atlantic coast, we had lunch at a restaurant on the beach, a wide sandy beach at the edge of the desert reminiscent of another beach of long ago. The loud Afrikaners at the next table, seemingly uneducated country bumpkins swilling beer, had nothing in common with the more sedate and sophisticated British with whom my unconscious peopled the restaurant. Embarrassment made me look the other way; I wanted to excuse this behavior to our native Namibian hosts, but they had lived with this for generations and didn't expect anything different.

After lunch, feeling unwell, I withdrew from the group that headed south to the enormous and impressive sand dunes, the "ski hills of the desert," a sight not to be missed, I was told. But nothing could induce me to go along. I wanted to be alone. We were housed at an Afrikaner Seaside Retreat whose surrounding barbed wire fence was a potent reminder of the South African era when Namibia was the fifth province of that country. Here the white population of South Africa had vacationed, well insulated from the local population. Once in my room I crawled under the blankets and shut out the world. I sensed that the memories might overpower me, might fill me with an unbearable nostalgia for a time I could never retrieve.

From Swakopmund we traveled north to the small town of Oniipa, stopping on the way to admire the wildlife at the Etosha National Park. In Oniipa, we were housed in a guesthouse belonging to the Namibian Lutheran Church.

The next morning I woke at dawn and dressed quietly so as not to wake the two women with whom I shared a room. I stood in the doorway to the courtyard eyeing the hibiscus trees that stretched their scraggly flower-filled stems towards the sky. All was quiet except in the kitchen of the guesthouse where the cook was getting the morning meal ready. I slipped through the gate, my sandals stirring up the dew-covered sand, and walked down the hill towards an empty, wide, and sandy river bottom. The sun was just rising and from nearby huts I heard the clanging of pots and pans.

As I walked up the *wadi,* I was wistful, my senses alert. So much was familiar: the starkness of the landscape, the smell of the sand, the whispering of tall palm trees, the thorny acacias, and the village waking to a new day. I was back in a different world: the world of my adolescence. Long forgotten memories flooded my interior, memories occupying recesses of my mind I had not explored for years.

Whatever my expectations had been, I hadn't known it would be like this: this was Africa, a continent separate from the world of my youth. I thought this would be a new exotic experience, not one that would yank me back into my adolescence.

And now here in Oniipa, a village in northern Namibia, as I walked in the empty riverbed surrounded by goats nibbling on the thorny bushes, I finally allowed the memories to well to the surface. I was no longer a fifty-nine year old woman in Africa, a recently retired physician. I was a young European girl in a desert country on another continent, on the other side of the equator…in Aden in Southern Arabia.

Later, during the long ride north toward the Angolan border, three of us in the van played a game called "tell me your life's story." The young girl who initiated the game had lived and worked in Namibia, if only for a year, and was eager to tell us of her short, but significant life. As a child she had lived as an expatriate American in South Africa. Her family was expelled from there when her father became too outspoken. And now she was back here, in the formerly annexed part of South Africa. The other American, middle-aged like myself, quietly and sympathetically gave us the highlights of his life. When my turn came I realized how fervently I did not want to tell them about myself. My emotions were at the surface. If I talked, I might cry. The memories were nothing but raw feelings. I could make no sense of them to myself, let alone to my fellow travelers. I sat behind the two storytellers, but leaned forward between them, as if to bridge the distance between middle age and youth, between considered eloquence and youthful nostalgia. I envied the young girl. She was so exuberant and filled with excitement at being able to re-experience some of her childhood. I too wanted to go back to my youth. But for me it was too late. The place where I had spent my adolescent years was gone; it existed only in my memory. I spoke haltingly, but it seemed to me that nothing I said made sense. I gave them the facts.

"I grew up in Denmark." I said this because, now an American citizen, I had lived in the States for more than twenty-three years and my accent was all but gone. "I was born there, my parents were Danish, as was my whole family except my Swedish grandmother." This statement always played well in Minnesota, my home state, where being of Swedish descent validated you as a citizen. "But my parents, who were missionaries, lived much of their life in Arabia. I lived there with them in the fifties, from age twelve to sixteen, and when I left, I knew I wanted to become a physician and that I wanted to return there to work. This never happened, and now I have just retired from my practice of neonatology." I told them about my husband and three children. There it was, my life story, in just a few sentences. I also told them that this trip was having an unexpected effect on me, an effect I was still trying to sort out. There were long pauses as I allowed myself to be lost in thought....

This trip became seminal for me in a couple of ways. First of all it was a catalyst for the writing of my coming-of-age memoir *Pearls on a String*. Secondly, while visiting the government hospital in Oniipa, I saw sick children and babies who reminded me of why I had become a physician in the first place. The seed I had unearthed within me during this trip finally found a place to grow. It wanted me to pick up on the promise I had made to myself when I was a young girl, to work in a developing country, finally fulfilling the goals and dreams of my youth.

23. On a Quest

On returning from Namibia, I began—at first in a desultory fashion—to explore a number of organizations that might need my skills. As I saw what the possibilities were, I explored with more intent and contemplated many different organizations. In the end, however, I opted to work as a volunteer for three months with the Evangelical Lutheran Church of America's Division for Global Mission. They indicated that the Lutheran Church of Cameroon was looking for a pediatrician for one of their hospitals. As I shared my intentions and research with Hans, he worried endlessly about my plans to go off to a developing country. Though I did my best to persuade him this was something I had to do, he remained unconvinced.

Before I left, I finished up my Masters Degree in Liberal Studies at the University of Minnesota, Duluth, and I made my last elective class a course on African history taught by a Congolese professor. I knew a little about the major countries in Africa, but knew nothing of the rest.

Cameroon's history indicated that the Portuguese had arrived on its shores in the 1600s, and because of the many prawns found there, they named the area Cameroon (prawns in Portuguese is camarões). The interior was not settled until late in the nineteenth century.

By this time, many European countries had explored and set up spheres of influence in Africa, and there was intense competition for exploitation of Africa's resources. Because of this a conference was held in Berlin in 1884, headed by the Imperial Chancellor, Otto von Bismarck. There, the political partitioning of Africa among European countries took place: what was later to be called *The Scramble for Africa*. The participants arbitrarily divided up Africa in ways that took no account of the natural borders separating tribes, something that would have significant consequences when the countries regained independence in the 1960s. In East Africa, Germany laid claim to Tanzania and Rwanda-Burundi, in West Africa to present-day Togo and Cameroon, and in southern Africa to Namibia.

During WWI, Britain invaded Cameroon from Nigeria. The last German fort in Cameroon surrendered in 1916. After the First World War, Cameroon was put under the mandate of Britain and France. Those two countries ruled Cameroon until it won its independence in 1961. The western part that had been under Britain used English as their *lingua franca*, whereas the larger former French colony used French. To the present day both languages are used, and media venues such as television and radio are bilingual. It is useful to have these two common languages, as there are about 220 tribal languages in Cameroon as well. The population in 1997 was 17 million in an area the size of Oklahoma.

Norwegian and American missionaries had set up missions in the Adamaoua highlands from about 1920. The missions had established schools, churches, hospitals, and clinics. All of these were turned over to the native Cameroonian Lutheran Church at some point after the country's independence, but there continued to be collaboration with the Lutheran churches in America and in Norway. I was to work in one of the three Lutheran hospitals, Ngaoundéré Protestant Hospital.

Through fax and telephone conversations with missionaries and people who had worked there, I received information about living conditions in Ngaoundéré and about the hospital. As I learned what might be needed in Ngaoundéré, I spent much time in my former workplace, the NICU at St. Mary's Medical Center, gathering equipment to take with me.

In late April of that year, a beautiful spring day beckoned me with promises of a bountiful growing season—and what holds more promise than the rare spring day in Minnesota? I looked at the garden. There was so much to do that I would not be doing this year. I would miss the nourishing Duluth summer. But I reasoned that whatever the season, there would always be regrets about leaving, so best get on with it.

On the day of departure, friends called to say farewell and others came to the airport to see me off. It was emotional saying goodbye to Hans, but I knew I would see him again in less than four weeks. As he had not been able to dissuade me from going, he had made the decision to take three weeks off from work to visit me in Cameroon and would come to Ngaoundéré in mid-June. I found that very courageous of him, as he would be traveling on his own, didn't know any French, and had never lived in a developing country. Christine, who had spent blocks of time in Central America, was also very interested in being with me for a while, and she would come in mid-July and stay with me until I returned home. Thus the three months would not mean a total separation from family.

As I later waited in Kennedy Airport for my flight to Paris, I took stock of my feelings. I felt apprehensive, had many doubts, but was willing to tackle whatever lay ahead. I felt there was a purpose to what I was about to do, and that it was not just a product of some romantic notion and willfulness on my part.

The plane from Paris to Douala was far from full. I had expected to be in the white minority, but there were very few blacks on board. There were some women who appeared to be missionaries, a lot of business-men, and young French families with children. I was reading Scott Peck's book *The Road less Traveled* and read the chapter on separateness in love. I thought that Hans and I practiced this well. We had always given each other the opportunity to develop and grow, to become the best we could. We did not see each other only in terms of what we could be for each other, though our togetherness nourished us and gave us strength and encouragement to be separate. Reading that chapter affirmed me in the path I was taking.

The plane made a stopover in Lagos, Nigeria. I took note of the fact that I had now visited the two airports in the world that the U.S. Transportation and Safety Board had deemed too unsafe to certify. Lagos was one, the other was Port au Prince in Haiti. The plane wrecks lining the runway in Lagos amply underscored this. I felt better once we were in the air again for the one-hour flight to Douala in Cameroon. After a night of sleep there I expected to arrive at my final destination, Ngaoundéré, early the next morning. Little did I know what lay ahead.

24. Douala, Cameroon

When I arrived in Douala that evening, I felt so enormously tired after the long flights that the expected onslaught of people in the airport failed to threaten me. I was just happy to have come this far. Sweating profusely, I had stood in line at the health booth, showing the yellow card that documented my yellow fever vaccination, without which I could not enter the country. Then it was on to passport control where a bored, indifferent, or maybe sick employee stamped my passport, and finally I was at the baggage claim area. Porters in green uniforms milled around among the passengers. One of them, Roland, who spoke English, attached himself to me. This proved fortunate, as my luggage had not arrived. He brought me to the baggage claim office where I filled out the appropriate forms. Then he took me to the hotel shuttle.

The drive to Hotel *Ibis* was scary and much too fast. Clutching my seat and the non-functioning seat belt, my heart in my throat, I thought, "I haven't quite arrived, yet I'm about to die in the streets of Douala." When the chauffeur slowed, I thought I could relax, but then, arrogantly, he ran a red light as he turned left to the hotel. This was one of few traffic lights in the country—Ngaoundéré had none. Cameroonians, I later learned, see no point in stopping for red lights if there is no cross traffic.

The *Ibis* is a little oasis in a chaotic city. It was a welcome sight after my long travel. It was clean, with good service, polite staff, very European; I felt reassured. It was past ten o'clock when I finally had dinner. After a fitful sleep, I woke to the alarm at what I thought was five o'clock in the morning but was in reality four. I had been unaware of the one-hour time difference between Europe and Cameroon—no Daylight Saving Time in the latter— and felt poorly rested. In the meantime I had an opportunity to call Hans who was at home worrying. When I paid my hotel bill a short time later, I found that the call had cost me an astonishing sixty-five dollars. The shuttle back to the airport for my seven o'clock departure was filled with a mix of white people: a French doctor heading for a conference in Yaoundé, business people, and oilmen.

I had made arrangements to meet Roland at the airport. There was no sign of him, however, and as I stood wondering what to do, an airport employee approached me, saying my luggage was downstairs. If I paid him 3,000 CFA (about $6), he would take me there. I said no thank you. I was not about to follow him into the bowels of the airport. He might have robbed me, stolen all my money, and taken my passport; and then again, he might not have. Better to stay where I was outside the airport.

The morning was amazingly cool and refreshing. As far as my eye reached, there was dense green forest. The sky was hazy, the sun large and a fuzzy red. I saw scattered run-down white houses, splattered halfway up with red clay from the rains; all had corrugated roofs. The smell of burnt wood pervaded the air.

Shortly after, Roland showed up. He confirmed that my luggage was indeed in Douala, and that it would be put on the plane for Ngaoundéré. Everything was taken care of. Next I needed a boarding pass, and there was nothing easy about that, since standing in line in an orderly fashion seemed foreign to people here. Roland helped.

Afterwards, I sat down with other passengers and waited to be called to the gate. Nothing happened for a long time. I congratulated myself on being patient. This was Africa after all, where nothing happens on time, and indeed it didn't. Meanwhile I ordered coffee and crepes at a small booth; service was slow, but both were terrific. Soon we were told that the plane would depart, not at seven but at ten.

A woman in her mid-thirties entered the departure hall. She quickly struck up a conversation with me, the only other white woman among the passengers. I learned that she was Carmen, a Swiss physician, who was flying to Maroua for a meeting on the same plane as I. She had been born in Cameroon, in Garoua, where her father had set up a textile factory, and she had lived there until she was sixteen. She loved the country. Already I felt a kinship with her. After moving to Switzerland she had become first a social worker, then a physician. Straight out of medical school she had returned to Cameroon and had gone to work in Ngaoundéré. She was now working for an NGO (non-governmental organization) in Douala.

Ten o'clock came and went; nothing happened. Carmen wandered around and chanced to see the plane surrounded by military personnel and vehicles, and wondered if the army was commandeering the plane. Elections were coming up in two days, and there was fear of unrest.

At noon all passengers were finally summoned to the restaurant where we were served dry sandwiches and told the plane was canceled due to technical problems, "technical problems" being, as always, a euphemism for "whatever."

By this time, Carmen and I had become travel mates. We tried to find out whether a plane would leave the next day, Thursday. There were flights north every other day, and Thursday was the last scheduled flight of the week, as all air traffic was canceled Saturday because of the elections. Our departure could therefore be as late as the following week. We got no answers, and Carmen decided to go back to her clinic. She suggested I switch hotels and move to The Tropicana, located next to her apartment, so we could go together to the airport the next morning or whenever there was a plane.

Her chauffeur brought her truck up to the entrance at the airport and Carmen heaved her backpack into the back of the pick-up along with my luggage. The chauffeur and the two of us crammed into the front seat. Leaving the airport, we made our way along the road leading southeast out of the city. The chauffeur constantly tooted his horn at people, dogs, goats, and other vehicles. A multi-colored throng of people surrounded us in what looked to me like a slum area, walking indiscriminately in the middle of the road despite the traffic. So many people, I thought. Most of them lived in houses made of cement-blocks with corrugated-iron roofs. Part of the road was lined with little "holes-in-the-wall" that hawked a variety of goods. There were beauty salons, tailors, liquor stores, and small general stores. But in other parts "open-air stores" spread their wares on the ground, with the vendors sitting under huge, variegated beach umbrellas selling shoes, peanuts, yams, pineapples, cell phones, toilet paper, whatever: small mom-and-pop stores under a canopy. Yet despite the obvious poverty many people were extravagantly dressed: the women in colorful dresses with equally colorful cloths around their heads. Many men were dressed in Western clothes, well-pressed pants and squeaky-clean shirts.

Our progress through this pot-holed obstacle course was characterized by stops and starts. There seemed to be no traffic rules, and in intersections the turning vehicles squeezed haphazardly between cars, goats, motorcycles, and people.

I felt dazed, as I had had little sleep since arriving in Douala. I marveled at the fact that I was riding through the slums of this dirty port city on the African continent with people I had just met, to a destination I knew nothing of, and yet I felt no anxiety. It was as if I had suspended all disbelief and worry, living in the moment, trusting that my protective angel, Carmen, would take care of everything.

We arrived at Carmen's clinic. She grabbed her stuff, and as she ran off, she told the driver to take me to the hotel. The driver became agitated and swore at her in French. Not understanding what he was saying, I was at a loss to know what was upsetting him. Maybe driving a white stranger around was not in his job description. I worried about adding fuel to the fire by speaking to him, so I said nothing except to tell him *merci beaucoup* when he finally, after a hair-raising ride, dropped me off at The Tropicana.

That evening, Carmen and I had dinner at a small local restaurant across the street. As we sat on an outside terrace in the still hot and humid evening, mosquitoes quickly and intensely launched an attack on my ankles. I had fortunately, as recommended, already started my malaria prophylaxis. The food was Cameroonian *ndolé,* a green sauce, made from a spinach-like green, with meatballs. It was tasty and spicy, and I knew right away I would love Cameroonian food. French wine was served. The dessert was French as well: *crème brulée.* In order to converse we had to shout at each other to be heard over the traffic noise from the street: a heavy circulation of cars, taxi-cabs, motorcycles, and pedestrians, mostly young men and women dressed in European attire, on their way to bars, the cinema, or eateries.

The next morning Carmen and I were at the airport at five thirty and learned there indeed would be a flight that day. There was mass confusion at the check-in counters. Everyone who should have been on the plane the day before fought to get to the ticket counters before this day's passengers. As Carmen was excellent at shoving her way through a crowd and making her voice heard, we quickly got our boarding passes. A mad scramble to get on the plane followed as there were no assigned seats, thus more pushing and shoving. The two of us managed to get seats together and by eight we were in the air.

I now found myself in a different world. The plane was old and shabby. Fulani men—tall and with Aryan features—had boarded the plane by the dozen. The Fulani (variously called Fula, Fulbe and Peuhl) are a nomadic people who populate the north of Cameroon and many areas across western Africa. They turned to Islam in the eighteenth and nineteenth centuries in order to have a more organized government and they eventually became very powerful as they spread Islam through *jihad*. Many had now settled in towns as merchants and were often quite wealthy. They were the predominant people of northern Cameroon.

These Fulani men who entered the plane were dressed in long flowing robes in white or pastel colors, beautifully embroidered, that lent them a quiet dignity. The few women onboard were gorgeously dressed in colorful silk or synthetic chiffon dresses with matching head wraps, yet despite their finery they almost failed to outshine the men. All passengers carried much luggage. What couldn't be stowed in overhead bins was stored under people's legs and in the aisle. In an accident, exit from the plane would be impossible, but maybe that was irrelevant as any plane accident in Africa was likely to be fatal.

The flight was fine, the pilots capable. An announcement at take-off stated the flight would go directly to the capital of Chad, Ndjamena—an unscheduled stop—and that it would land in Ngaoundéré on the way back to Douala, extending a two-hour flight into six hours. I soon learned that in Cameroon, flights go where passengers need to go and schedules are not necessarily adhered to.

Finally three days after leaving Duluth I was about to land in Ngaoundéré in the Adamawa Province of Cameroon.

25. Culture Shock

As we approached the airstrip in Ngaoundéré, I glimpsed the landscape where I would be living for the next three months: a lush green savanna with scattered trees and isolated mountains. The plane landed smoothly, rushing past yellow buildings, slowing by a small plantation of eucalyptus trees: a reforestation project, I later learned. It taxied back and the passengers disembarked onto the tarmac, picked up their luggage, and proceeded in single file to where a mass of people waited outside the small airport. Fellow tribesmen ceremoniously greeted the tall Fulani men, and the women, in all their splendor, were enthusiastically met by family members.

An older American missionary identified me, picked up my large duffel bags loaded with equipment, and drove me to the mission compound about five kilometers from the airport. Garbage dumps, with goats grazing happily on refuse and plastic bags, lined the road. Ngaoundéré was then a city of over 100,000, yet mud huts with grass or tin roofs seemed to suggest a village.

We entered the mission compound via a long avenue of shady mango trees, and passed schools, church offices, and single family dwellings before pulling up to the tiny house, incongruously called *le chateau*, that would become my home. It was like a small cabin in the north woods of Minnesota. With a cement floor, it was not luxurious, but it was perfectly adequate. I decided I would sleep in the larger of two bedrooms. It contained a double bed, a makeshift closet, and a chest of drawers. The tiny bathroom had a shower with a gas instant hot water heater and a flushing toilet. The small living/dining room had a couch, two single arm chairs, a dining table with three chairs, all made somewhat crudely of wood. In the small kitchen were an electric refrigerator, a gas stove, a sink and a huge homemade water filter. The house sat on a little knoll with a large shady eucalyptus tree to the east. Everything was small, but I was thrilled.

Exhausted after the long journey, fraught as it had been with mishaps and uncertainty, all I could do was stretch out on my bed for a while.

That evening I was invited to have dinner with Karen Noss, an American missionary whose husband Jim, the station manager, was traveling that day. Karen had Ravel's *Bolero* playing on the stereo, its endlessly repetitive motif blaring out into the rapidly darkening African evening. Karen and Jim's home would become my safe haven, the place I would go to unload when I was frustrated. They both always listened patiently and helped me with advice. Jim's parents had been missionaries in Cameroon and he had spent his childhood here. He had returned when newly married, and their children, now adults, had grown up here. Jim spoke French and several tribal languages fluently, and had keen insight into the Cameroonian mindset. He was a wiry man, constantly on the go. Karen was immutable; nothing fazed her.

After dinner I went back to my small "castle" and went to bed, overcome with fatigue. Grateful to be at journey's end I contemplated my stay here and wondered what the next three months would bring. What was I doing here? I felt very ambivalent. Eventually I went to sleep under the canopy of a mosquito net and slept for twelve hours.

I had arrived in Ngaoundéré at the beginning of the rainy season, which lasts from May until November, and during that first night I experienced a violent tropical thunderstorm with rain pounding on my roof. I would find that these storms often occurred late in the day or during the night. The ground was drenched with rain in the morning, and the red clay road had turned into a small river. The night had been surprisingly cool and I had been compelled to put on tights and socks to keep warm.

In the cool, early hours of the morning I set out to discover my surroundings. I found the compound eerily familiar—very like the Swedish mission compound we had stayed at in Ethiopia the year I turned fourteen—and with this recognition, I realized that part of what had brought me here was a longing to relive the experiences of my adolescence. As before I was aware that the carefree days of childhood had lent a special quality to those reminiscences, something that as an adult I could only recapture in memory.

The compound covered thirty to forty acres, and was dotted with approximately fifty houses surrounded by swaths of grass and shady trees. With the arrival of the rainy season the withered scruffy grass on the large lawns had sprung to life and was now very green. As I passed by the house of my next-door neighbors, another missionary couple, I saw them having breakfast in an open *bouqarou*, a large grass hut, in their back yard. The goats grazing around another house seemed to indicate that it was occupied by Cameroonian employees, and then I passed a guesthouse outside which, in tall pines—planted by Jim's father—I heard the loud buzzing of African killer bees, and saw them swarming, exposing their long, trailing legs. Later, on a trip in the bush, we stopped and had lunch under trees that housed a beehive and I was stung by one of the African killer bees. I had expected the physical reaction to the sting to be exceptional, but much to my surprise it was no worse than had it been a local bee in Duluth, Minnesota.

I passed Jim and Karen's house, next to which was another rambler occupied by another missionary. Across from them was The French House. It had earned its name by the fact that this was where French nurses and French volunteers stayed. In France, you could get an exemption from military service if you were willing to work in some capacity in a developing country, specifically in former French colonies. Most of the young male French volunteers taught at the church's high school.

As I explored further, I passed a field where young people, Cameroonians and Norwegian volunteers, played soccer. I passed the Norwegian missionary houses, the school for Norwegian missionary children, and the beautiful old colonial house that now belonged to the president of the Cameroonian Evangelical Lutheran Church. Next to it was the Church Headquarters. After passing other Cameroonian employee housing, I came to the quaint, small, red brick church at the entrance to the compound—made from the red clay of the region— that had been built by the Norwegians half a century or more before. I tried to imagine those pioneering missionaries as they built the small church for a small growing flock of Christian converts. Could they have imagined that nearly 50 percent of the population would now be Christian? And could they have imagined that around the turn of the next century a Millennium Church would be built next to the small church that would house two thousand people? Nearby were the two-story buildings that were the Lutheran Church's high school for both boarding and day students.

A six-foot wall surrounded the entire compound. Shady trees graced the entire area: lush mango trees heavy with fruit; lacey jacaranda and flame trees; avocado trees; spindly frangipanis with strongly scented flowers; and colorful hibiscus trees and oleander bushes. Ngaoundéré is situated on the Adamawa Plateau, at 3,500 feet, and has a pleasant climate despite being only four degrees north of the equator.

In 1951, my family and I had spent a summer vacation and my fourteenth birthday at the Swedish Mission in Harar, Ethiopia. Our stay there had been such a welcome change from the hot dusty weather of Aden. Harar, a Muslim city in that Christian country, lies at 6,000 feet and according to the explorer Sir Richard Francis Burton—one of the first Westerners to visit there—the weather during his short residence in January of 1894 reminded him of Tuscany's. We, too, found the climate pleasant and it was a particular balm for my mother who had been worn down from illness. She recovered readily there as she relaxed, free from housekeeping duties.

We lived in a white guest cottage, not unlike my house in Ngaoundéré. As always when my parents, my sister and I vacationed away from Aden, we spent the days hiking and reading, my father reading aloud to us at night. Often he read Dickens, an author he and we loved.

This was also the summer I began studying German since I needed that language for my continued studies in Denmark. My love of languages was nurtured during those years. I kept Danish alive by speaking it to my parents. English was spoken at school, with my sister, and with my European friends. I spoke Arabic with our only servant Abdullah, a young boy my age, in the market, and with other Arab friends. I had been studying written Arabic during the preceding year.

Harar enchanted me by its lushness and profusion of tropical trees and flowers, and it was here I made my first acquaintance with mosquito nets. Like the icing of a fairy tale castle cake, the net fell in folds around my bed and enclosed me in a world of my own. In Aden—due to scanty rainfall and the use of DDT—there were no mosquitoes and malaria had never been a threat. My sister, father, and I hiked every day in the surrounding mountains and valleys. Our plan had been to go to the higher altitude of Addis Ababa after a few weeks, a goal that was thwarted when my mother sprained her ankle.

That second evening in Ngaoundéré I had dinner with Dr. Simon Aroga. He was a young Cameroonian doctor at the hospital who had just returned to Cameroon after finishing medical school and an internship in Germany. Having somewhat of a problem communicating, as my French was halting and his English likewise, we compromised by speaking a mixture of German, French and English. With an engaging open manner and an infectious smile, he seemed congenial and anxious to please. He had just moved into his assigned house, a white house built of cement bricks with a corrugated iron roof, containing a couple of bedrooms, living/dining room, kitchen, and bath. It was one of many employee buildings around the hospital. As he was unmarried, his two sisters lived with him and cared for him. I was surprised that the table was set for only two. We dined alone, waited on by the sisters. I was amazed at the food: rice with chicken in a mildly spicy sauce, accompanied by a dish reminiscent of spinach, different from the one I had experienced in Douala, accompanied by a drink, *folleré,* made from dried hibiscus flowers. For dessert there was pineapple and papaya.

A few days later, his colleague Dr. Salpou, also a young physician, trained in Cameroon, stopped over at my house to say hello. He had just returned from a training course in birth control in Douala. He had a wonderful smile, was soft-spoken, and seemed conscientious. These two young doctors would eventually become our best Cameroonian friends.

The next morning the secretary at the Hospital Direction, a Belgian woman called Madame Brigitte, took me around the hospital. It was quite large and spread out, housing about two hundred patients and consisting of a number of buildings. Some were old patient pavilions that were built in the forties. With stone foundations and walls, they were quite solid, but the windows were small and the patients liked to keep them closed, resulting in a very dark hospital room that accommodated three to four patients. There was no running water, and toilets were at the periphery of the hospital compound. The newer buildings included the laboratory, the x-ray facility with machines dating to the fifties, surgery, and maternity. The outpatient department was also a recent addition. Everything, the pavilions especially, was far more primitive than I had imagined, and filthy. Their patient rooms were like dungeons, painted dark brown. The dispensary, the maternal-infant clinic, and the maternity ward were cleaner. My immediate impression, however, was that to practice medicine here would be impossible. Seeing the supply room's minimal inventory only confirmed this for me.

Because of the confluence of elections and the National Holiday around a weekend, I had several days to myself to get adjusted in my house. On Sunday I went with Jim and Karen to the English language church in town. With us was a young optometrist, Bob, who had arrived a few days after me to do a similar volunteer stint at the eye clinic. The congregation catered to Christians from the English-speaking part of the country in West Cameroon. A young American seminarian was a temporary pastor and gave a spirited sermon. Interestingly, a translated summary of the same sermon in Pidgin English was given immediately after. Though the congregation consisted mostly of English speakers, they apparently did not all understand American English. I was completely bowled over by the finery of the women: colorful embroidered outfits consisting of blouses with puffed up sleeves and *panga* skirts. Most wore a fabulously convoluted headgear more characteristic of Nigerians, and possibly some of the women were Nigerian. The men were dressed in kaftans, reaching mid-thigh, and pants of the same color. Some were dressed in European clothes. The singing in this church would not impress me as the singing in the hospital church later would. A young man who was obviously just learning to play the keyboard would belatedly strike up the tune after the congregation had started singing, and always in a different key.

Outside of Madame Brigitte's introduction, I had no orientation to the hospital, but when work finally resumed at the hospital after the holidays, I was quickly put to work. On my first day I was plunged head-long into seeing patients and left to fend for myself. Before I knew it, I was making rounds on the entire pediatric in-patient ward. Surprisingly, there were no hospital charts. Each patient had a so-called *carnet*, which was their property and in which healthcare providers seeing the patient, whether here or at any other hospital, made notes. Both physicians and nurses authored these scribblings, since nurses in many cases functioned as nurse practitioners. The *carnet* was where I was to write my orders and my impressions of the patient. It was slow going as I labored to interpret the previous entries in the *carnet*: brief commentaries, scrawled in ink in an illegible French. I had boned up on my high school French by taking classes at the university the spring before coming here, and had also acquired a book with French medical terms, but my French was as yet insufficient. As I was unable to communicate with the patients directly, the morning became a frustrating experience. It was helpful that both male nurses rounding with me knew some English, but even had I spoken fluent French I would still have had to rely on second-hand information since many families spoke only *Fulfulbe* or another tribal language.

I experienced my first malaria cases, first TB case, lots of gastroenteritis and malnutrition. I pondered the lab order *G.E.* that appeared on every *carnet* and learned it stood for *goutte épaisse*, the "thick smear" test for malaria, where the blood is examined under a microscope for the presence of the *falciparum* organism that causes malaria. The test was ordered on most patients, as malaria presents with so many faces. The lab was unable to do many of the tests I requested, most notably cultures of any kind.

The patients were adorable, many of them very sick. The mothers were often beautiful, young Fulani women. Each of them had taken up residence in their child's bed, a twin bed, the surface of which was woven rope and merely covered with a piece of cloth, quite uncomfortable. On this second visit to the hospital I must already have become desensitized to the dirt. In my involvement with the patients I failed to notice it.

The hospital did not provide food for the patients, which meant I could do little about malnutrition if the mother could not afford the food. The hospital did, however, have a nutritionist who taught mothers what to feed their infants once they were weaned from the breast. Though breastfed babies are usually chubby and healthy looking, they quickly become malnourished once weaned, because they are often fed only manioc (cassava), a high-carbohydrate root with few other nutrients.

Nurses' functions were to start IVs, give IV medications, and instruct in, though not give, care. Families were the caregivers and gave all the oral medications. At first I thought this was a good solution to nursing shortages, in that it allowed parents and family to have responsibility and control. I later realized that it resulted in disaster and poor treatment outcomes. Parents only bought oral medication for a few days at a time because they had so little money. When the child got better, the parents failed to see a need to continue medications, they refused to renew the prescriptions, and often they left the hospital against medical advice with a partially treated child. In the adult wards lack of nursing care had the same ramifications, and often meant that the patients were not kept clean or repositioned regularly, resulting in bedsores and avoidable infections.

Almost all of the employees of the hospital were members of the Evangelical Lutheran Church, which owned the hospital. They were committed Christians, yet surprisingly they didn't always show Christian caring toward their patients. This was an issue that would perplex me for years.

At the end of rounds that first day I had been sweating buckets as the hospital had no air-conditioning. I was also thirsty and hungry since it was now one o'clock. The hospital had no cafeteria, and as regular working hours were from seven to two, I called it a day and retreated to my house for lunch. After lunch I rested. Feeling overwhelmed I contemplated what I had gotten myself into and I asked myself what I thought I would be able to do here. Hans had not wanted me to do this. I had insisted, but I wondered: had it been the right thing to do? Why was this so important to me? Would I be able to do meaningful work here? I continued to feel very ambivalent.

A few days later I visited a younger missionary. Luther Symonds and his wife, Nusrat, were Canadians, she Pakistani-Canadian. They had three adorable young kids. We discussed the situation at the hospital and they talked of its problems. In their opinion the hospital wanted a white doctor like me working there only because I attracted more patients and thus generated revenue. They said I should abandon the notion that I could teach anyone anything; no one was interested in learning. This was discouraging to hear, yet before coming here I had felt there was so much I could do, the most important of which was to teach the doctors something. If the missionaries were right this might, however, also be the most difficult task.

26. More Culture Shock

While frustrated at the hospital, I enjoyed my little *chateau*. In the afternoons when I came home I often took a rest and then sat outside the kitchen door reading. Women and children came by selling me fruit: the juiciest pineapples, which I learned to know were ripe by their yellowish color, mangoes, papayas—which I didn't care much for as I had been fed too many of them in my childhood—the small four-inch bananas that were heavenly, carrots, beans, lettuce, green peppers, and what have you; it was a bonanza of local superb-tasting fruits and vegetables.

In Cameroon the only significant weather change relates to rain. There were six months of nourishing rains and six months of absolute drought. In the rainy season everything grew exceedingly well. In the dry season, most agriculture rested, but later, while visiting in the dry season, I would see many small plots along the river with dense rows of vegetables, watered from the river.

I had wanted to experience more of the town, but the American Embassy had warned Americans to stay away from crowds around the time of the elections where president Biya was elected into office for the third, fourth, or fifth term, I knew not which; a questionable landslide victory.

Once things settled down I decided to walk into town to get groceries, as I didn't have a vehicle. The compound was on the outskirts of Ngaoundéré and *le centre commercial* was about three kilometers away. I passed by mud dwellings with tin roofs clustering along the road, but soon I was in town where the houses lay side by side, only interrupted by streets and alleys. Here and there were large compounds surrounded by walls, inside which were large mud huts with grass roofs, as well as several more modern buildings. Those compounds looked well kept and appeared to belong to wealthier people. All alleys and many roads were only dirt roads, though some streets were paved.

As I made my way I noticed there was little traffic and only few people about. The lack of throngs should have been a warning. I had not worn a hat and soon I became dizzy and felt overheated; the sun was right above my head. I looked for a place to get out of the sun, but there was none. I wondered what would happen if I fainted in the street. Would someone pick me up and bring me to the hospital? I stopped for a little while under a lonely mango tree, but felt such intense thirst that I knew I had to find some place soon where I could get something to drink. All stores were closed, but finally up ahead there appeared a café with a shady verandah. I staggered in there, asked for something to drink, just anything, and was handed a fruit drink of a kind. I knew it might not have been prepared with clean water, but at that moment I couldn't have cared less. I sank into a white plastic chair on the verandah and sat there savoring my drink while cooling off. An older man came by, and taking pity on me, stated the obvious, "It's very hot. You should not be walking outside. Where is your hat?" Indeed, where were my hat, my water, and my common sense? I felt utterly chastened by my stupidity, and when I had recovered I was able to hail a taxi to go back home; no shopping for me that day.

This became my first experience with the ubiquitous taxis. There were exceedingly many cabs, I would learn. All were yellow and in various states of repair. The driver rarely drove with a full tank, but added gasoline periodically by buying one big coke-sized bottle of it at a time from vendors on street corners. And you did not get to have a taxi for yourself. The fare was one hundred CFA, the equivalent of a quarter, and the cab was shared with others picked up along the way and dropped off as the driver went by their destination. Thus I had the company of men and women, packed into the taxi, sometimes five in the back, two in the front, and I got a tour of the town before the driver finally dropped me off at home. People rarely talked in those cabs, either to me or to each other.

From then on, I took taxis to go shopping. I frequented a store owned by a Lebanese family. It had much canned food and other necessities, but also fresh French cheeses and chocolates and French wines. Nothing was cheap there, as almost everything was imported from Europe. I also learned that stores were closed from noon until three or four in the afternoon, a sensible arrangement considering how hot it was in early afternoon.

The mornings at the hospital began with devotions in the chapel that all employees attended. This was often followed by an address by one or other of the employees regarding certain goings-on at the hospital, changes in procedures, special events and so on. At times there were lectures. On one of the first mornings, Dr. Daniel Salpou and one of the nurses, Madame Frida, gave a report on a conference they had attended in Douala on birth control. They talked about the new methods that now would be offered at Ngaoundéré Hospital. Most often women came alone for birth control, but at times husband and wife agreed together that they had had enough children. This mainly happened with well-educated people. The hospital had so far offered contraceptives in the form of pills, shield, and condoms. What was now to be introduced was injectable contraception that provided months to years of contraceptive effects. I listened as the nurses and doctors discussed this new method, and then to my astonishment, Dr. Yadji, a surgeon, said, "This is just another way for the white people to control the population of Africa." He sounded angry and combative. This gave me food for thought. Cameroonians, like most people in Africa, prize children. Children are what will sustain the parents in old age, and with the high infant mortality rate and increased mortality in the general population, having many children was a shield against reaching old age without any support. Yet these frequent pregnancies exhausted women and led to higher pregnancy losses. As Dr. Salpou pointed out, spacing of pregnancies would lead to healthier pregnancies. I guess Dr. Yadji let his prejudices against whites override his logic.

Then I was off making rounds with the male head nurse in maternity, Benoît. We were getting to know each other. Benoît spoke reasonably good English and we could have conversations about patients. He was a man of medium height, with coarse features, a broad smile, and a loud, hearty laugh.

On our rounds we stopped by a mother who was doing well, but whose baby, born prematurely four days before, was in poor condition. The baby appeared dehydrated and I wanted to give him IV fluids.

"We don't put IVs in newborns," Benoît said.

"We don't? Well, we will now," I said, though I wondered aloud if there was a cultural taboo against needles in babies, but he assured me there wasn't. The very dehydrated three-pound baby lay quietly in his mother's bed, his limbs splayed, his cry weak, and his eyes rolled back in his head, as if it were too much of an effort to keep them focused. He had not been able to suck, and the mother's milk had not come in. The nurses had given only water, by gavage. I told Benoît what I needed and he explained to me that the mother had to go to the pharmacy first to buy all these things, and only if she had the money could we put an IV in the baby. After a long while, the mother came back from the pharmacy with the IV glucose, but no tubing. Had she had no money for it, or was this an oversight by the pharmacy? There was another trip and finally, almost two hours later, I got an IV started and glucose running as well as antibiotics. I ordered the rate for the IV, but when it became evident there was no IV pump, I worked for a long time with Benoît to impress upon him the need to watch the IV closely to ensure it didn't run faster than the rate I had set. I left the child in the makeshift overhead heater in the hallway.

I had just reviewed maternity's records for neonatal deaths: fifteen babies out of 100-150 born per month had died, a mortality of 10 percent or greater, with the average weight of the ones who died being 2000 grams (four pounds eight ounces). This little baby I was now seeing would likely die too.

Thereafter, I went to the prenatal area where I encountered another challenge: a seven-day-old infant with marked jaundice whom I admitted to the maternity ward.

"Do we have phototherapy with which to treat the baby?" I asked Benoît. Yes, he said, he thought so, but since he had only been in charge of maternity for ten days, he didn't know where everything was. We hunted around for the phototherapy; bulbs were in one place, the unit in another. We placed the baby in the simple cot made out of cardboard. The bili lights were mounted too close to the child, but there was nothing I could do about it; the baby needed phototherapy. Fortunately the maternity ward also had eye shields. The bilirubin must have been exceedingly high, probably over thirty as the baby was more orange than yellow, but we had no way of measuring the level. I got back a hemoglobin level of five, from which I concluded he was hemolyzing. I managed to get blood for the baby. This was not as simple as it sounded, because there was no blood bank. Fortunately there were many relatives around; one of them had a compatible blood type and was willing to give blood. I could, however, place neither an umbilical artery nor a venous catheter for an exchange transfusion, so I had to content myself with just giving blood to the baby through a peripheral IV.

As I worked I contemplated whether the baby was septic. He seemed to bleed from puncture sites. I also entertained the diagnosis of disseminated intravascular coagulopathy, but the baby was not sick enough for that; he cried vigorously. I felt in a terrible quandary. I couldn't get the tests needed to make a diagnosis. All I could do was to treat his bilirubin and low hemoglobin. I felt horrible not being able to do an exchange transfusion now that I had blood. I pondered doing a cut-down of a femoral vein, which might have worked, but I was unwilling to risk the procedure considering my concerns about his clotting ability. In this situation, less intervention was the best action. I didn't know his underlying illness, so I had no idea what his outlook might be. If he had disseminated intravascular coagulopathy, he would die, in which case all my efforts would be futile.

When later I thought of the day's experiences, I realized I had gone through so many conflicting emotions. Happiness at seeing and taking care of patients, frustration at the impossible situation of trying to do something to help the-small-for-dates infant survive, and uncertainty about whether doing so only would postpone his death. If the mother could not breastfeed him, the child would most certainly die. In the developing world, formula is supplied only as powder to which water has to be added; using formula invariably leads to gastroenteritis because of unclean water. Of course the mother would be instructed to boil the water, but would she always be able to observe sterile procedures?

Within twenty-four hours the baby expired; he became apneic, opisthotonic, very stiff, with a gaping mouth, edematous, almost scleremic. These are symptoms and signs we rarely see in the U.S. anymore, because babies are prevented from getting that sick. I decided to discontinue everything and just let the family care for him until he died. Over the next several days, however, I would find that the child with jaundice improved, and when I saw him back after discharge he was doing well.

This was really one small blessing, but still I felt I needed some affirmation that being in Cameroon and doing what I was doing was the right thing, but no affirmation was forthcoming.

One evening after having had dinner with the always-welcoming Jim and Karen Noss, I stepped into a two-foot-deep rain ditch in the dark and banged myself up badly. It shook me up; for though I acquired only a massive hematoma on my left thigh and a sore—broken?—rib, I couldn't help thinking, "What if something more serious had happened? Was there the medical expertise here to deal with a pneumothorax or a fractured hip? Could I die here because of an illness improperly treated?"

Just as I was about to go to bed that night, a guard from the hospital appeared. I was wanted. A child with a hemoglobin of two and a diagnosis of chronic anemia exacerbated by malaria needed an IV. I struggled for four hours, but could not get one in. The poor child! I wanted to call someone for help, but as I was called as a last resort, at least that was what I assumed, there was no one to call. I felt completely defeated as I walked home at two in the morning.

She was still alive the next morning when Dr. Nagbata was able to put in a subclavian line. It was beyond my expertise to do that, I had therefore not attempted it. I felt such happiness that she would likely improve with blood and might walk out of there that I didn't speculate on why I had been called to see the patient without the doctor on call, Dr. Nagbata, first seeing her. Later on, I became convinced that I had been sent for because Dr. Nagbata had refused to get out of bed.

Days at the hospital usually started with a radiology conference immediately after chapel where all the five doctors were present. Besides the two young doctors, Dr. Salpou and Dr. Aroga, there was Dr. Nagbata, a knowledgeable person who did only what pleased him, Dr. Yadji, a surgeon who suffered from exalted feelings of self-worth, and a Malagasy doctor, a quiet and self-effacing man who mostly covered the outpatient department. The doctor going off call reported what had happened during his watch. After the radiology conference one morning, Dr. Salpou asked all the doctors to come to the maternity ward, where I had the opportunity to lecture them on trisomy 13/18 and hyperbilirubinemia. I was elated that they all came. Maybe Luther Symonds wasn't right; maybe people really wanted to learn.

These happenings during the first few weeks left me on a roller-coaster-ride. I had not counted on experiencing such emotional turmoil. But I resolved that I would make myself look at my situation in a positive light. Maybe it was important not to think so much about whether I could make a difference. I might just have to look at these first weeks as an adjustment period, learning the ropes. And, I wondered, could I possibly learn to function without all the resources I thought I needed? Maybe.

27. Unable to Help

My alarm went off. I abruptly emerged from a dream whose content I had already forgotten. I reached for the small flashlight under my pillow. The alarm showed 5:15 and it was still pitch black around me. As the torch illuminated the translucent mosquito net falling in billowing clouds around my bed, I lay back trying to orient myself. Though I had already been here for two weeks, my first inclination when I awoke was to think I was at home in Duluth Minnesota. But the minute I felt or saw the net, I knew where I was. As that realization set in, I thought about my tenuous situation here: were my efforts of value and were they even wanted?

My line of thought was intruded upon by the recollection that this Sunday was the morning for the picnic. I untangled myself from the net, stepped out onto the cement floor, and pulled the string for the ceiling light. It illuminated my double bed with its mosquito net, a bedside table with a back-up kerosene lamp (matches next to it), and an open closet that contained a hanging rod and the few clothes I had brought. I went into the minuscule bathroom and turned on the shower where the in-stantly-heated very hot water invigorated my mind and body. Irene and Marianne, two nineteen-year-old Danish volunteers, would take me out for a breakfast picnic on the mountain this morning.

I was dressed and ready when they knocked at my door. I locked up the screened porch as I left. With the help of flashlights we found the road that passed between houses whose occupants were still asleep, and then traversed a gate in the six-foot walls that surrounded the com-pound. In the dawning light, we discerned a path in the red dirt, winding down toward a stream. Cautiously, so as not to step on snakes, we parted the eight-foot-tall grasses and banana palms and finally crossed the small river, balancing precariously on a single narrow board. The morning was cool and glorious, the countryside quiet. No one stirred yet in the adjoining grass-thatched mud huts. Dawns here are so abrupt that within minutes, as we made our way along the cassava crops into open fields, it became light. To the east, the mountain beckoned us. The path was lined by fields of millet and cassava, interrupted periodically by the presence of mango trees.

When we reached the mountain fifteen minutes later, we followed a path going steeply upward. Slipping because of gravel on top of red clay, we clawed at and held on to the tall grasses. We stopped at a huge flat boulder, the picnic site. Marianne and Irene were volunteering high school graduates who brought no special skills, but did odd jobs around the mission compound, presently as nannies for a Norwegian and a Danish missionary family. The girls had brought fresh baguettes bought at the market outside the compound, yogurt, and coffee, and I contributed butter and cheese: a Danish breakfast on a soon to be sweltering African morning.

A haze enveloped the sun, which rose as a huge fireball, quickly diminishing as it continued its steep ascent into the sky. The fields came alive. On the path below us, adults and children pitter-pattered, ran, skipped, or walked sedately on their way to market carrying vegetables, fruits, and firewood on their heads. A man climbed past us to his cornfield further up the mountain. He was unfazed by the presence here at this hour of three white women. Through the awakening morning we heard the muted thrusts of a hoe and the distant reveille from the army barracks a mile away. We sat talking in our communal ancestral language, sharing stories of how our lives' trajectories had brought us here, while people on the path below shouted greetings at us: *Bon jour. Ça va?* Or the Fulani greeting, *Sanu, djamna?* We stayed there till about nine-thirty in easy communication as we watched and heard the locals start their day.

Returning to the compound in the heat of the day—the sun had climbed so high its rays were burning—we were met with the penetrating fragrance of the large pinkish-white or yellow flowers of the frangipani trees, while the flamboyantes, the vividly red flame trees, and the blue jacarandas provided shade from the now intense sun. It was Sunday morning, and people on their way to church passed us dressed in all their finery, the women in colorful or white embroidered dresses with fancy headscarves. Conceited young girls teetered on high heels. The relaxing hours I had spent on the mountain in the company of compatriots had erased all my concerns about patients and my reasons for being at the hospital, but as I got closer to my house I saw a woman standing by my door.

"The baby is not well," she said in English. "Please come," she pleaded, as she bent toward me, her palms together. She was the mother of one of my preemies, William, and I hastened with her to the hospital. This was 1997 and there were no cell phones in Africa. As I didn't have a landline in my house, the only way to find me was to go looking for me. No emergency response was possible. I was surprised that the mother, and not a nurse, had come.

William had been born three days before and weighed three pounds twelve ounces at birth. He had been stable in the mother's bed, dressed in the thick pastel knits people indulge in here—imports from France, I presumed—and had been kept warm with gloves filled with hot water and wrapped in cloth. Since hot water was not readily available—there was only cold water in the three existing taps in the maternity ward—William had not always been kept warm enough. In order to get hot water the mother or her sister had to go to the family kitchen in another building to heat water over an open wood fire. She had breastfed him when he had been strong enough to suck; otherwise she had expressed milk directly into his mouth (the old French method of the Couney baby shows). He had looked healthy every time I had seen him, with good color and turgor; his belly had been soft.

In order to examine the boy, I took him from the mother's bed to a makeshift cot by the delivery rooms. It had overhead heat and light from a balanced-spring heat lamp. A dangerous situation, I thought. I was distrustful of the springs; were they to give way the lamp would fall on the baby creating enormous burns. I undressed him and found his abdomen quite distended. His color was mottled, and I was sure his blood pressure was low. I asked for oxygen. As always, the nurses struggled to make the compressed-air machine work.

There was no doubt William had developed necrotizing enterocolitis. In this environment he could not survive. He had started vomiting late the night before. No one had notified me so I had known nothing about this until the mother appeared at my doorstep. I felt discouraged that nurses here had no sense of urgency. I knew things come on fast in newborns, but how could the nurses not have seen that William was so obviously sick? The mother knew, and the nurses must have ignored the mother's assertions. I didn't need an x-ray to confirm the diagnosis. I had seen it all too often before. Besides, taking him to be x-rayed would destabilize him further and would be helpful only if I planned surgery, which I did not.

Necrotizing enterocolitis is a condition where the gut becomes compromised and sometimes necrotic (dead) because of decreased blood flow to the intestines, which can happen for a number of reasons. It is common in preemies that have been stressed either by cold, infection, or a difficult delivery. I had not been at the delivery. The mother's chart had only sparse notes, and no one who had been present owned up to any problems. It was a common story: not only was the hospital without adequate or appropriate medications, it was also almost impossible to get an accurate history, or any history at all. No one seemed to pay attention to the little clues that patients give. I started an IV and antibiotics, but I was not hopeful. William appeared to be in septic shock, though I could not document that. I had a blood pressure cuff, but no manometer. I could not even get a blood sugar level, let alone blood gases. I had no medicine to treat the baby's attendant acidosis, low blood pressure, or impending disseminated intravascular coagulopathy.

I explained to the mother what was going on. Most mothers who delivered here spoke only their tribal language and Fulani, and I could not communicate directly with them. With this mother, however, I had no problems since she was a well-educated English speaker from western Cameroon. She told me that since nothing could be done, she and her sister wanted to take William to their ancestral home in Bamenda in the Northwest Province that same night—first on the train to Yaoundé and then by bus from there, a two-day journey—so he could be buried at home.

As I had no hopes for the baby, I didn't oppose her wishes. She wanted William to survive until they got home and I had to tell her that he would surely die before. She understood. The stoic calm with which so many women here accepted that their babies might die amazed me daily. But the fact that one in seven children died before the age of five years must surely have induced a certain fatalism.

I was frustrated because, in the United States, I could have treated William. We would have taken him to surgery and given him appropriate post-op care and intravenous nutrition until he could feed again, and he might have survived. That was not possible here. We had a surgeon, Dr. Yadji, but his qualifications were questionable. If I had been called the night before, maybe then we could have considered surgery, but not now.

I could not help telling the mother that had this happened in the U.S. we might have been able to save him. Maybe it was cruel and selfish of me to tell her that, and did I do it only to exonerate myself? Educated people here must surely know how disadvantaged they were. As I talked to the mother I felt increasing remorse about not checking on William more often, though that might not have changed the outcome. Yet, I defended myself...I could not remain in maternity twenty-four hours a day. That was what would be required to avoid disaster, since here I had no well-trained nurses to be my eyes and ears and no one to notify me of early signs of impending disease. I felt my specialized skills were worthless here.

When the mother decided to leave, I went back to my little house. There was a blooming century palm growing up against it. Blooming only once in its lifetime, it then dies. I thought about that: you arrive at your most significant achievement in life and when that is accomplished, you die: no second chances.

I entered my porch and was met with the sight of large one-and-half-inch-long cockroaches. Mice, snakes, and lizards don't bother me, but "critters" disgust me. Sometimes they crawled over my feet when I sat writing at the hospital at night. Poison traps had been put out for them in my house two weeks prior to my arrival and during the first few days I had found their corpses everywhere with their feet in the air reminding me of the nightmarish story of Gregory in Kafka's *Metamorphosis*. Huge crickets, flying erratic courses so you couldn't predict where they would land, assaulted me when I came in through this screened entryway at night. Apparently they got in through an opening under the roof. I couldn't unlock the door to the house fast enough to escape them.

I pondered the day's happenings, beginning with the incredibly beautiful morning and ending with the impending death of William. I continued to be on an emotional roller coaster. The feelings I experienced were largely generated by the experience of tragic losses of babies that would have survived in the U.S., compounded by feelings of missing my family and having no one with whom to reflect on my experiences. My specialty is a highly technological one, an expensive venture into the frontier of saving babies that fifty years ago, even for us in the Western world, would have been deemed unsalvageable. One could rightly question whether it was a frontier that any nation should have afforded to conquer. But we in the U.S. were there now, and retreat was impossible considering the expectations today's neonatology had generated for families in the West. I didn't anticipate anything like that for Africa in the near future, but much could be done with fewer means, and some babies that died here could be saved at a fraction of the cost we expend in the West.

This was my third week in Cameroon and I realized I was still in culture shock. I had thought I was prepared to witness all the illnesses and misery because I had seen it all before as a young girl. But then I had not been aware of the therapeutic possibilities that here were rendered almost useless by the enormous lack of resources, the nursing personnel's ignorance or indifference, and their ready acceptance of the futility of treating babies. The gap between healthcare in the developing world and in the Western world had only widened as technology had advanced medical care.

Something else was brought home to me: that I could not function without well-trained nurses. They were an extension of me, and I thought with gratitude of all my nurses back home. They were the essence of the care delivered, the reason for our success in the NICU.

Though I would feel little sense of accomplishment at the time, I would learn many things during my three months in Ngaoundéré, but nothing would become more evident to me than the enormous need for education and a changed mind-set about medical care.

28. Affirmation

During the night there was an insistent knock on the door. I stumbled out of bed, half-awake. A tropical rainstorm had hammered the roof for hours and must now have stopped or I would not have heard the knock. Outside was a man dressed in rags. He told me he was one of the guards at the hospital and that a nurse had asked him to get me. That a nurse should have sent for me was a surprise in itself. I was wanted for a child, a three-year-old with severe breathing problems. I had been here not quite three weeks. No one had told me about the hospital guards. So why did I trust this man enough to leave the compound with him? He was not someone who induced trust; nor was he threatening. I don't know why I went with him into the night, except I felt it my duty to go.

I learned later that guards were employed by the hospital to prevent thieves from entering patient rooms in the otherwise unattended pavilions. No walls surrounded the hospital compound, and anyone could have direct access to patient rooms, day or night. The guards were not effective, however, and patients locked themselves in at night, preventing the nurses from observing them. As I found out that night, the hospital guards also served as messengers, getting doctors to the hospital when needed during the night.

The mission compound where I lived had guards as well, and I heard them at night resetting a clock on the outside of my house to document they had made their rounds. Six-foot walls—later to be increased to eight feet with glass shards—surrounded the mission compound. Gates in the walls allowed admittance during the day, but were locked at night.

The moon slid behind clouds as we left my house. I had with me the outsized Maglite with three D batteries. I had bought it in the United States, thinking it could serve the dual purpose of lighting my way at night and being a defense weapon, in the unlikely event that someone should assault me.

I followed the guard to the big gate, which the mission compound guard opened for us. We crossed to the street outside and made our way to the hospital. Occasional streetlights along the road washed the luxuriant mango trees in a silvery sheen. The two-foot deep rain troughs were swollen with rainwater and were uncovered; I stepped with care.

We went to *l'acceuil*, the reception, a room with green paint that showed signs of wear and poor maintenance. The walls, table and floors were in need of a good scrubbing. It functioned as an emergency room and contained a table covered with white oilcloth. On this lay the three-year-old, a pale-gray, anxious boy, Abdoulaye, who expended all his efforts on breathing: the spaces between his ribs retracted as the sternum was pulled close to his spine with every breath. The nurse had already found an oxygen-concentrator and he was getting oxygen, though not enough considering the blueness of his lips and nail beds. The father hovered over his son.

Keeping his head still, Abdoulaye followed me with wide-open eyes as I moved around the room. While I listened to his lungs, he let go of his fear and let his eyes roll back in his head. I heard his respirations clearly, especially on the right and maybe less well on the left. There were no râles or rhonchi to suggest pneumonia or bronchitis. His father said the boy had not coughed. I suspected a pneumothorax, air that has escaped through a leak in one of the lungs into the surrounding closed thoracic space. One would normally expect to hear decreased breath sounds on the affected side, but in young children that is often hard to detect, as breath sounds are well transmitted even when there is air around one lung. I asked for a chest-x-ray.

"We don't do x-rays at night," the nurse said. I fought the irritation rising in me. An x-ray was essential if I was going to be able to do anything for this child. I was also annoyed because I had already been told more than once, "We don't do it like that in Africa," suggesting two standards of care: one for Africa and one for the rest of the world. This nurse was someone that I had not met before as he worked outside the maternal-child units. His arrogance and lack of concern for his patient astounded me.

It also surprised me that people in medicine here could be so stuck in their ways. I would later realize that they felt—and were indeed—harassed whenever an expatriate doctor got exasperated because of the lack of expertise and resources, as if it were the fault of the nurse who had the misfortune to be working with the foreign doctor at that hour. They feared the doctor looked down on what they had to offer, though *they* knew that they provided the best care in town. And they did: the care received here was much better than what was provided at the government hospital just a mile away; personnel there worked when they pleased and plundered the hospital for resources, so that none were available for patients.

I asked why they didn't do x-rays at night.

"Because the x-ray technician is not here and we don't have the key for the x-ray room."

"Well, how about if we call him in?" I realized the foolishness of this request the moment I said it. The technician, of course, didn't have a phone at home; landlines were not common and often not functioning, and cell phones belonged to the future.

"Can we send someone to get him?"

"He lives far away."

"How about sending one of the guards?"

"The technician doesn't like being woken in the middle of the night."

"That could be, but we still need him."

I continued to wheedle, reminding the nurse that Abdoulaye might not be alive by the time the x-ray technician came in the morning. I got no response. With time, I would find that people often find it safest not to answer an irate foreigner. They are not spoiling for a fight.

I sat down and started mulling things over. If I had a non-invasive transilluminator like we had in the NICU in Duluth, Abdoulaye's thorax would light up if I put it to his chest, but I didn't. I could put in a chest tube on the side where I suspected the pneumothorax and I would know immediately if my suspicion was correct: air would come whooshing out when I poked through the intercostal muscles. I didn't like that approach. It would be an unnecessary procedure if I were wrong, and I still wouldn't have an x-ray to tell me what the lungs looked like, and I still wouldn't have a diagnosis. But if I didn't do something Abdoulaye would suffocate. Fortunately, I had brought some chest tube trays with me from Duluth with all the sterile instruments I needed, as well as chest tubes and Heimlich valves. I decided to go home to get my equipment.

When I came back I saw that my patient was gone, as was the nurse. I started to panic. Had the father taken Abdoulaye away since I hadn't been able to offer anything, despite my having told him I would be back? Or had his son died while I was gone? I didn't think that was likely; he hadn't looked like he was tiring. The nurse reappeared and told me Abdoulaye was in the process of getting an x-ray, but offered no explanation of how that came about.

I went to the x-ray department, which was now miraculously open, and a technician handed me a film. It was not well exposed, but I could easily see that my presumptive diagnosis was correct. I was relieved, because I had the means to do something about a pneumothorax. Had something strange and unexpected turned up, I would have had to face yet another challenge of looking for resources to treat it; meanwhile Abdoulaye would have continued to deteriorate.

The father carried him back to reception. While in the x-ray department he had not been getting supplemental oxygen, because the heavy oxygen-concentrator, despite its wheels, really wasn't portable and he was quite blue by now. We quickly got him back under oxygen and I began the procedure.

I had providone-iodine swabs at the ready. I injected a local anesthetic that fortunately was included with the tray, and with a knife I cut a small hole in the skin. I tunneled the curved forceps above the rib and popped through the intercostal muscles, dilating as I went along. Removing the forceps, I passed the sterile chest tube through the hole I had created. I soon was in the space between the lungs and the chest wall. With a large syringe, I aspirated fifty cc of air through a three-way stopcock, confirming the diagnosis. I then attached the Heimlich, a one-way valve that lets air out but not in. The valve kept fluttering with every breath, indicating that air continued to move out of the space around the lung. Abdoulaye now breathed a little easier. Putting a suture through the skin and around the chest tube, I stitched it in place. I started an IV and antibiotics. Then I went home to bed.

In the morning, Abdoulaye was breathing easily and his father was effusive in thanking me for saving his son. I would not have thought that putting in a chest tube could make me so insanely happy, but for once while here, I had been able to do what I do well. Until now I had been in too many situations where my expertise was for naught because of lack of resources or lack of skilled nursing care. Despite difficulties, I had been able to do what was needed for this boy.

I was not able to determine why he developed the pneumothorax in the first place. He could certainly have had tuberculosis, but that seemed unlikely. He looked very healthy otherwise and had had his BCG vaccine—not foolproof, but his sputum proved TB-negative.

Over the next couple of days I got what was available of the lab work I needed. All was fine. A repeat x-ray after the leak had sealed revealed normal and clear lungs. After removing the chest tube I sent Abdoulaye home and hoped for the best.

This episode seemed to change my perspective on working at the hospital. I had gone through periods of doubt about what I was doing. I had felt I had nothing to contribute in this setting, but now I had the affirmation I needed. I loved neonatology because it allowed me at times to snatch babies back from the brink of death, a magic I had not been able to work here, at least not thus far. With this older child, the situation was different. Because of his age, his situation was less precarious and he was more resilient than a newborn. I liked working in tense situations where I could do something concrete to turn things around, but for that, I really needed a supportive medical team. I didn't do well at using diplomacy to convince patients with chronic problems to undergo treatment, nor did I excel at inducing uncooperative nurses to cooperate. Despite the initial lack of cooperation from the staff, this episode made me feel that I was able to accomplish some things and maybe even save some lives.

No one had ever put a chest tube in a child here, so this was a milestone for the hospital. The surgeon, Dr. Yadji, and the nurses wanted to know how many chest tubes and Heimlichs I had with me, and could they please have them. It was as if this were a magic wand—an instant cure—they would like to have in their arsenal. Though I demonstrated (to as many as cared to listen) how to make the diagnosis of pneumothorax and how to place a chest tube, for now I decided to keep my equipment for myself until I left. I would need it in the unlikely event that I would be called for another pneumothorax in a child.

29. Communication

I spent part of my days at Ngaoundéré Protestant Hospital in the Mother-Infant-Clinic. This clinic was located in the basement of the maternity building. Pregnant women came there for regular prenatal checkups and children came for vaccinations. Sick children were also seen there and I saw many of them. Since office space was at a premium I shared a room with the nurse, Madame Frida. My French was improving and I could now take a history from those parents who also spoke French. I enjoyed working in this part of the hospital.

This day I was faced with a petite Fulani woman who was extremely shy as are many Muslim women. She had arrived here on the back seat of a motorcycle taxi holding her two-year-old daughter, Amina, in her arms. Her three-year-old son came with her as well, seated in front of the driver on the gas tank. Not speaking French, she talked to me softly in Fulfulbe, using a body language that told me that Amina had been "hot" and had been vomiting. With repetitive signing of someone sleeping—head tilted onto her hand, eyes closed—she indicated the girl had been sleeping excessively. Maybe body language was the best way to communicate, I thought, since I couldn't hear her anyway in the surrounding noise: the chatter through the open door from women in the waiting area, children crying, and Madame Frida instructing a mother about birth control.

Amina's mother was dressed in her finery for the occasion: a yellow chiffon-like skirt, a matching top, and white sandals. She wore jewelry of orange gold. A yellow shawl circled her skinny oval face with its high cheekbones, straight nose, and light skin. Not crying, but appearing anxious, she looked down at the daughter in her arms. The boy stood quietly at her side. I motioned for her to lay Amina on a table I used as an examining table. The little girl was hot, unconscious, and did not respond to stimuli; her neck was markedly stiff. Her lungs indicated pneumonia. She didn't appear overtly malnourished. Her fontanel, still open, bulged slightly. All of the findings suggested meningitis. I attempted to get the attention of the nurse, "Madame Frida, excuse me, we need to do a spinal tap."

"We don't do that here in the clinic. That will be done in reception. Just write your orders, and everything will be taken care of there."

Madame Frida was a friendly, heavy-set woman with a ready smile. Like most nurses here, she was confident in her knowledge, which included practices that I did not agree with.

"You have to give antibiotics," she said when I got ready to send a patient away who had a viral infection. I explained to her that that would not make a difference in the course of the patient's illness as viruses don't respond to antibiotics.

"But you have to give the patient something. You can't just send her away with nothing. Give her some multi-vitamins at least." I was unbending, and on more than one occasion I saw her slip prescriptions to patients I had seen, because I wasn't practicing medicine "the African way." "We don't do it like that in Africa," was her constant refrain. Nonetheless, she came to consider me her special friend.

"Would you please tell Amina's mother that her daughter has meningitis and needs to be hospitalized and treated? Also tell her she needs a spinal tap."

In pediatrics there is a strong need to be reassuring when communicating with the family, but I could offer nothing because I didn't speak the language. So I cringed when I heard Madame Frida's harsh tones with the mother. I couldn't tell what she said, but she might well be scolding her for all I knew. The mother said nothing, just folded her shawl across her face and looked down. Then as she nodded, I realized I had understood one of Madame Frida's words: *"Fahem?"* "Do you understand?" an Arabic word also used in the mother's language of Fulfulbe.

I wrote the orders in Amina's *carnet* and sent mother and daughter on their way to reception.

A few hours later I found that I had been much too trusting. When Madame Frida had told me that all admission orders would be taken care of in reception, I had assumed she had told me the truth, and technically she had.

I walked to reception to find out where Amina had been admitted. There were no phones in the hospital, and every day I spent a lot of time walking around, trying to find staff I needed to talk to. To my surprise, I found Amina still lying on the single examining table in reception. Her mother sat by her, appearing more wary than before. No nurse was present. By asking at neighboring nursing stations, the responsible nurse was tracked down. No spinal tap had been done, though the IV and ampicillin had been started. The child's clinical status was the same. I introduced myself to the nurse and asked, "Why wasn't the spinal tap done?"

The nurse just shrugged. He had just come on. Nobody had told him a spinal tap was to be done.

"Didn't you check the *carnet*?"

"I haven't yet."

I was about to tear my hair out. Here was a child deathly sick with meningitis and no one had cared to perform the single most important diagnostic test, even though the nurses were very skilled at doing spinal taps. Normally we like to get the tap before antibiotics are started so that we can be sure to culture whichever bacterium is causing the infection, and so that the sensitivity of the bug to a range of antibiotics can be determined. Now, however, I was forced to take some consolation in the fact that at least the antibiotics had been started as ordered. After a lot of hunting around, iodine and sterile two-by-twos were located, the spinal needle was bought from the pharmacy, and I was able to do the spinal tap. The spinal fluid was cloudy and a subsequent Gram-stain showed Gram-negative bacteria. Since the lab couldn't do cultures or sensitivities, I would never know the cause of the infection or which antibiotic was best, so I merely made an educated guess: most likely the meningitis was caused by hemophilus influenzae— a common cause of Gram-negative infection. I chose to change the antibiotics to chloramphenicol, because that was what we had here that hemophilus influenzae should be sensitive to; it was like shooting in the dark. So, in fact, my great concern about getting cultures and sensitivities on the spinal fluid before starting antibiotics was a moot point, as none of those tests could be done.

By the next morning Amina was slightly better, her temperature lower, and she responded somewhat to stimuli. I followed her closely to be sure the antibiotics were continued. Her improvement was gradual and one day when I went to see her, she was gone. I fretted over this, not understanding how the nurses could have let her go. I was told families often make such decisions without communicating them to the staff. Amina was better, she had no fever, and her family concluded that there was no purpose in spending any more of their precious resources.

If only the population were more knowledgeable about diseases, I thought. If only people had more money for medical expenses. If only the staff were more insistent on teaching families the need for finishing a course of medication…those were all the "if onlys" that were driving me crazy as I was learning to treat patients here. I adhered strictly to the way we practice medicine in the West, and that was my goal for how things should be done here.

Shortly after this, I met Dr. Daniel Brobeck, a stout Germanic-looking man in his early thirties from the Alsace-Lorraine area of France. He appeared to have the same attitude as Luther Symonds: people at the hospital were not interested in learning. With time, I came to believe that it was the Western person's obligation to help people become interested in learning.

Dr. Brobeck had worked at several of the Cameroonian Lutheran Church hospitals and had a lot of experience in this setting. With funding from Norway, he now ran the church's primary health project, which entailed going to villages to vaccinate children and teach mothers about appropriate prenatal and newborn infant care, while following all the newborns for at least a couple of years to be sure they grew and developed normally. This was a great program that within a few years was turned over to a Cameroonian, Lambert Bouta, a public health nurse. Under his management it continued to do well, as I saw on a trip I made to the bush with him in 2005. That is, it did well as long as there was funding. When the funding from Norway ran out, the program died a slow death. As it wasn't generating money, it became unsustainable. This is typical of many programs started by foreigners in the developing world.

Daniel Brobeck confirmed to me the day I met him that physicians from the U.S. or Europe tend to become discouraged and angry, just as I had, when patients leave the hospital, terminating their treatment. They are liable to lash out at the nurses, whom they see as indifferent or maybe even in collusion with the patients. I don't think that Daniel had gotten beyond the point of being angry with the staff, which is where I was at this point, and I think he exemplified the struggles all Westerners have when working in a developing country, especially when working in a hospital or health institution run by local people. With time, I came to realize that the nurses know that those incidents—patients leaving the hospital without finishing their course of treatment—are part and parcel of practicing medicine here, and they have a more relaxed attitude about the inevitability of it. But this, in turn increases the Western physician's suspicion that nurses don't care, so it becomes a vicious circle that tends to increase the distrust between staff and the volunteer Western doctors. I eventually came to gain some insight, but it didn't prevent me from feeling demoralized every time a patient disappeared before treatment was completed.

I came to see Daniel Brobeck as a real bush doctor. His wife Clarice was a petite French nurse who assisted him with the project. She managed to live and work with him for a couple of years—traveling the bush in a jeep doing important public health work— before she gave up and they divorced. For years after, we continued to see Daniel's name crop up in Cameroonian contexts. He continued to work elsewhere in Cameroon, as it seemed he was not ready or willing to settle down at home in France. Africa had gotten a hold on him.

30. A Farm in Africa

Hans arrived on the 10th of June, four weeks after I had left home. His trip until he arrived in Ngaoundéré had been uneventful, and he came bounding down the boarding steps eager to see me, scanning the welcoming crowd for a blond white woman but seeing none. Collecting his luggage on the runway, he walked toward the yellow airport building; still, I was nowhere in sight. Little by little the passengers left with their families; he alone remained at the airport. He had no phone number to call, could not communicate with airport personnel as he spoke no French, and there were no cabs at the airport.

Meanwhile, I was on the way to the airport, riding with Luther in his pickup truck. On the road past the railroad station we saw a barricade up ahead. This was nothing unusual. Police often stopped traffic at checkpoints, purportedly to check car papers and IDs. Every person in the country is obligated to carry an ID at all times, and we carried copies of our passports. When we got to the barricade, a drunken policeman approached us with a gun, and soon enough we realized that this checkpoint was only a ruse to extort money. The policeman asked to see our papers and the car papers. They were duly submitted. He pretended to find something wrong with them and insisted that we pay a fine. Luther refused and pointed out to him that the papers were in order. The policeman became more insistent, but the more combative he became, the firmer Luther was: he was not going to pay. It was a standoff. Time passed; soon we had been there for half an hour. We would become used to these stops, and much later, at a time when bandits were rampant, we would experience being stopped repeatedly as we traveled up north. The police were trying to flush out the bandits. As banks were dysfunctional at the time, people often traveled with large sums of cash they were transferring, being creative about where they hid them in their cars, and we, as foreigners, were also presumed to be in possession of readily accessible wealth, making us the target of bandits as well. Finally, however, on this day, the policeman unhappily conceded defeat and let Luther and me go. Soon we were at the airport, much to Hans's relief.

Hans shared my delight in my little house. I felt more anchored with him there. He had insisted that he wanted to see patients while he was in Ngaoundéré, and before he arrived, the church's radio station was supposed to have announced that a gastroenterologist would be available at the hospital. Somehow this didn't happen, and the first day he found himself making rounds with Dr. Nagbata, as there were no gastroenterology patients for him to see. He was as disturbed and depressed as I had been at what he saw that first day. But soon patients were standing in line to see him and he became totally enchanted by the population. He felt they provided such a contrast to many patients in the United States, who seek medical advice with the slightest complaint whereas here, most patients were legitimately sick, many of them desperately so.

We both found that the Cameroonian people were incredibly hospitable and friendly, their smiles so welcoming that we thought them the most amazing people in the world. Only among the nurses did we find some resistance or occasionally even hostility. Hans quickly, as he usually does, befriended a patient and his family, and one day we found the patient, a man, at our doorstep with food for us. He came in and we sat down for a meal together: meat in a spicy peanut sauce, fried plantains and manioc. We grew to love the different Cameroonian sauces; the meat, however, especially if it was beef, was sometimes quite tough. Manioc is hard to love for people not used to it. It is a staple of developing countries because it is drought-resistant and grows on marginal soils. To us, it had an unpalatable consistency and an odious taste, but it's something Cameroonians long for when abroad, like northern Europeans long for potatoes, and Italians for pasta. We later learned that there is a bitter and a sweet manioc. The bitter variety contains cyanide, and must be soaked in water for three days to extract it, then squeezed, dried, and crushed before it can be made into a flour for couscous: a cooked glob of a gray, gooey substance the size of a softball, from which one twists off a portion with the fingers as one eats. It is very high in carbohydrates, and contains calcium, phosphorus, and vitamin C, but no protein. I assume this was sweet manioc. We politely ate some of it, but gravitated to the very tasty fried plantains. Women and children, the ones lowest on the food chain in developing countries, will, if they are starving, sometimes eat bitter manioc before it has been soaked thoroughly, and then become sick from it. Some women have permanent nerve damage and goiters from consuming cyanide in manioc over many years and I would see many children with Kwashiorkor—protein malnutrition— due to an exclusive diet of manioc.

The first Sunday morning Hans was in Ngaoundéré, we went to church at the hospital compound. The church there was an octagonal building with slatted windows on six sides, built perhaps twenty years before. We were happy to find an almost empty pew toward the front. Within the first ten minutes after the service began, people were filing into the church in droves. Soon all the pews, including ours, were crowded. We were shoulder to shoulder and could hardly move. As people entered, several youth choirs took turns singing, one of them directed by a young boy of about ten. The rhythms of Africa are intricate, beguiling, and difficult for foreigners to emulate, but the little boy had them down pat and the teenagers in the choir followed him. Every person in each choir had outfits made of the same cloth, the women's a blouse and a skirt, the young men's a shirt and trousers. They swayed their bodies to the rhythms, their smiles infectious as they sang. Soon women and men from the congregation came dancing up the aisles and in appreciation of the music placed a 100 CFA coin (about a quarter) on the foreheads of the singers. Because they were sweating slightly, the quarters stuck to their skin. Then followed singing by the congregation, the usual liturgy, and a sermon. The choirs sang again during offerings and communion. We always felt uplifted by the Cameroonians' enthusiasm for singing and by their strong Christian faith.

A few days before, Daniel Brobeck had invited Bob, an optometrist, also a volunteer, Hans, and me for lunch. Daniel and Clarice's bungalow in town was very tastefully decorated with African artifacts and furniture, and they had a cook who prepared a delightful lunch for us. Since Bob was an avid big game hunter, the conversation turned to the one person in the Ngaoundéré area who was the master and facilitator of the great African Hunt: Jean Vannier. The next thing we knew we were invited to Jean Vannier's house in the country.

Daniel and Clarice picked us up in their old Renault one Sunday morning after church. We could have gone by taxicab, but we thought the Renault might be safer. Taxis in Africa are poorly maintained and the road taking us north was recently rebuilt with smooth blacktop, inviting daredevil speeds. The Renault, however, was as ill-maintained as most taxis, and Daniel's driving just as bad. Add to that his love of speed and it is understandable that Hans, Bob and I not only worried about an accident, but were also certain, on several occasions, that we were going to hit another car. Accidents on Cameroon's roads can be ghastly and often lethal, if not immediately, then soon after as emergency response barely exists.

As we left the main road and made the gradual climb to the Vannier farm, we also left the traffic behind. It was a beautiful day and spectacular vistas opened up around us here on the Adamaoua Plateau. Tall grasses were interspersed with occasional acacias, mangos, and palms, and large rocky outcroppings and picturesque villages made the landscape enchanting. As always in Cameroon, the air carried the smell of smoke from villagers cooking on open fires; added to it was the odor of dung as cows grazed freely. Though we were sweating in the warm, humid weather, a breeze through the windows of the car made us comfortable.

The farmhouse was a low structure, built by French colonialists in the 1920s, sited at a high point surrounded by huge mango trees that provided blissful shade. A bright purple bougainvillea climbed a huge *kapokier*, the *ceiba* tree that produces kapok. The silky yellowish-white strands of the fruit constitute the moisture-resistant kapok, which was previously used in life preservers and as stuffing in furniture. From my childhood I remember mutilating dolls stuffed with kapok by plucking at their innards. Of course now, with newer, more cost-efficient artificial materials available, there is no demand for kapok anymore, yet when we later entered the old farmhouse I was told that all the cushions contained it.

Rita and Jean Vanniers welcomed us and walked us to the front of the house where poinsettia trees and rose bushes framed the view over the valley to the east. Here, in clear weather, one could see for a hundred miles. I imagined Karen Blixen, portrayed by Meryl Streep in the 1985 film *Out of Africa*, standing here saying, "I had a farm in Africa..." There was a patio from which one entered the main room, simply furnished with old colonial tables and chairs, African carvings, paintings, and photographs. The windows had no screens, just bars and shutters, although some windows also had glass. Was it too cold for mosquitoes here at this altitude? A fireplace heated the house in the evenings. A gorgeous painting of a naked African woman caught my eye. Jean had bought it twenty years before, he said, from a local painter named Abesollo. The picture entranced me, and as I was interested in buying African art, I asked Jean if he knew where Abesollo lived. He said he had lost touch with him.

The Vanniers were an unlikely pair in today's African bush, a throwback to colonial times. Jean was a short, trim, and fit man, dressed in khaki shorts, Rita petite and as elegant as if she had just walked out of a Parisian fashion house. It was incongruous that they should live here in total isolation and under primitive circumstances. They had electricity from six in the morning until nine at night thanks to a gas generator. They pumped water from a nearby river and stored it in a water tank. There were no TVs, telephones, fax, or computers to complicate their lives. They loved the solitude and quiet. All they could hear were the birds and the occasional cow lowing when she had been separated from her calf.

They served us appetizers of fried peppers, baguettes and pâté, then veal, potatoes, and salad—with red wine, of course—followed by a mango torte. They told us about their lives. Rita had lived in Cameroon since she was six, and Jean had lived here for forty years. I suppose he had come here from France as a government employee when Cameroon was still a colony of France; they were now probably in their early sixties. When they had first moved to the farm some twenty years before, they had 2,500 sheep that Rita cared for while Jean was gone on safaris. Jean Vannier was a big game hunter, but no trophies adorned his house, though there were plenty of hunting photographs. They showed macho hunters posing triumphantly by dead Lord Derby eland (a very large species of deer), lions, elephants, hippopotami, harnessed bushbucks (a pretty variety of striped deer), western roan antelopes, and warthogs. Jean's hunting camp, made up of several large *bouqarous* (grass huts), was also pictured and appeared quite comfortable. Bob, who was from Montana, hoped to go hunting while in Cameroon and he listened with fascination to stories of his host's numerous safaris. Jean expressed concern that poaching and unlicensed hunting might destroy the entire animal population in Cameroon, and told us he had made reports to both the French and Cameroonian governments stating that if excessive hunting was not curtailed there would be no large animals left. Poaching in the national parks was now seriously prosecuted. Years ago, the government had given Jean access to a large area in northeastern Cameroon where he brought white hunters for sustainable hunting during the season that ran from December 15 to the end of May, later curtailed to January through the end of April. A two-week hunting Safari cost about $9,000 per person.

As I contemplated the photographs on the wall, I could not help thinking how distasteful it was to shoot these magnificent animals just to satisfy white men's primordial hunting instincts. I am not keen on hunting, but understand the need for it in situations where an animal population gets excessive, such as in the case of deer in Minnesota, and also provided that hunters actually eat their prey. But this hunting of magnificent African animals for their antlers only angered me, and I wondered who ate the deer meat here. Was it just thrown away so the hunters could take their trophies (antlers) home or was it given to local people to eat?

The issue of hunting elephants is a very touchy and much discussed topic because often the elephant is hunted for its tusks only. In 2012, poachers from Chad flew into one of Cameroon's national parks in helicopters, and before Cameroon's police and army were able to get mobilized to chase them out, they managed to kill three hundred and fifty elephants for their tusks to sell in China. This almost makes you cry. Yet much of the poaching in Cameroon is carried out for meat, for sustenance. As a consequence of this so-called poaching by locals, there is no longer any wildlife in the Ngaoundéré area. Maybe I don't understand sustainable hunting, but I couldn't help thinking that if Jean was so concerned about the survival of the magnificent animals of Africa, why shoot them at all? In view of our hosts' graciousness in inviting us, I refrained from bringing up this topic. Though I liked the Vanniers personally, I had difficulty coming to terms with Jean's livelihood.

Rita no longer handled sheep. That had become too much for her to handle, so they now had 1,500 head of cattle, which were less work, though they had to be put through a bath of insecticide every two weeks to kill the tsetse flies. Rita handled this labor-intensive work with only a single helper.

Obviously, they had two lucrative businesses. They had an apartment in Paris and a house on Côte d'Azur in southern France. The oldest son, Franck, helped Jean in his business, but one wondered how long they could continue with the farm.

As it happened, we were to return to Cameroon on many more occasions, and over the years we would see the Vanniers in passing, usually as one or the other of us were getting on or off a plane, or when Jean loaded his boxes with trophies to be sent to his European or American clients.

We again saw them in 2009 when Rita was sick. Hans took care of her. She now looked older and frailer, but as courteous and elegant as ever. Jean had also aged and had trouble getting in and out of his jeep. They still lived on the farm. Rita still cared for the cattle and while son Franck had taken over most of the business, Jean continued to be involved in leading the safaris. They had conceded to technology by having a cell phone. Jean called me conscientiously over the next couple of days to tell me how Rita was doing. Neither of them spoke English, so I would speak to him in French and pass the message on to Hans. She was getting better, no more fever, he said. On the final call he told me she was back to normal.

31. Mbé

After visiting the Vanniers' farm, I better understood the French farmers who had put down roots here. The landscape was beguiling, especially during the rainy season, grazing was plentiful, and there had been excellent opportunities to make money because of the low cost of labor. The standard of living was good and often better than what the farmers might have had in France. After Cameroon gained its independence, thousands of French remained here, but over time they were made to feel unwelcome and eventually most left.

Ngaoundeba Ranch, south of Ngaoundéré, was a reminder of the lost glory of French colonialism. The Ranch had functioned as a resort for colonialists. We went there for lunch one day. It had a main stone lodge that featured a lounge with a beautiful stone fireplace and a restaurant; the furniture was French rustic with an African theme. The Ranch, however, had fallen on hard times. No one was staying there anymore and the attractive *bouqarous* stood empty. The minder of the place scrounged to come up with enough ingredients to serve us dinner, yet he was able to serve excellent French red wine. After lunch we followed a path to the nearby crater lake. Its deep waters had seen many swimming parties in past times as the lake was supposedly bilharzia-free, but we were not tempted: rumor had it that a crocodile was now in residence. Surprisingly, I found that the water-filled crater had the beauty and grace of a Minnesota lake.

Luxury was near unobtainable for the indigenous people. A chosen few, however, had wealth of enormous proportions. This sort of wealth almost always required a pipeline to the ruling government or directly to the president. In Ngaoundéré the richest Cameroonian was in the process of building a mansion at the top of a mountain with marble floors, swimming pool, and a private mosque, all with an imperial opulence. His wealth derived from maize production: he had been given access by the president to thousands of acres of farmland where he grew corn using modern farming techniques, tractors, and the latest in harvesting implements. To ascend to such wealth seemed like attaining the American dream. Yet the common man understood that this was for the chosen few only, and that it required special connections.

Even though some native people might have considerable tracts of land, and though they might be able to afford a used tractor from the U.S., access to state-of-the-art farming equipment was not within their grasp. Customs charges, taxes, and transportation would have made this impossible.

In visiting a former Norwegian mission station in the village of Mbé—eighty kilometers away—we received another glimpse of how whites can live comfortably here, at minimal cost. Invited by the only remaining expatriate presence there, a young couple from Norway, we set out from Ngaoundéré at 3,500 feet and with a pleasant climate, to Mbé, closer to sea level and very hot. The trip involved negotiating *La Falaise*, the escarpment that is the border of the plateau to the north. Driving in one of the mission trucks, Hans was initially anxious about traversing the escarpment, but with good brakes it proved less intimidating than anticipated. The many truck wrecks in the gullies along the road, however, bore evidence to the fact that the road was treacherous. Trucks in Cameroon are often old and are always overloaded. Poorly maintained brakes put them at a distinct disadvantage on this steep road with its many S-curves. Much too often, drivers lose control, careening off the edge of the road, and are pitched to their demise.

After having been forewarned of stalled trucks by branches strewn on the road, we passed several. One of them had been stopped in its too-rapid descent by the rock wall on the right side of the road. Others had simply broken down. We watched with fascination as drivers attempted to fix transmissions and whole engines they had lifted out of the semis and onto the road. If spare parts were needed, the drivers might sit there for weeks until replacements were obtained.

Shortly after we got to the bottom of the escarpment we found ourselves in the village of Mbé with its many mud huts. The heat was oppressive, but within a short time we were seated in Dag Tormod and

Janne's cool and spacious home. Beautifully and tastefully decorated with local art, it had wide verandahs back and front and honeysuckle framing the entrance to the house. With its white walls and red roof, it had a very colonial feel. The young couple and their son Mattis were welcoming, and after we had filled ourselves with water and cold juice, we were ready to explore the outside.

Dag fussed over dinner as Janne took us for a walk into fields that seemed to stretch forever across the valley to the mountains far away toward the east. Three-year-old Mattis accompanied us and chatted away in Norwegian to his mother while speaking Dii to people we met. In the fields, the nurse who managed the local church health center was plowing his soil with the help of a small tractor, made available to him through the church's agricultural program; it was the only tractor we saw in Cameroon.

At dinner, Dag served a Lord Derby eland roast cooked to perfection, fried sweet potatoes, regular fries, a lentil salad, gravy, pickled beets, lingonberries, mango for dessert, and then chocolate and coffee. We had not experienced such an elaborate or delectable dinner since coming to Africa. Dag talked about his work as a pastor for several rural Lutheran churches, and Janne, a graphic designer, about her efforts to encourage printers in Ngaoundéré to use local talent to illustrate books instead of illustrations that had no connection to the local culture. In this context we talked about how unfortunate it was that France had long had a monopoly on schoolbooks for the country, resulting in Cameroonian school kids reading about and seeing illustrations of blue-eyed, white children to whose lives they could not relate. This was about to be remedied.

Later we were shown to a guesthouse surrounded by hibiscus bushes. With no electricity the kerosene lamps shed a warm glow on the living room as I sat down to write in the diary I incongruously kept on my laptop computer (until I ran down the battery). The guesthouse had a flush toilet and showers with cold water.

In the relative cool of the next morning we took a walk in the village and returned to a fabulous breakfast: homemade bread, homemade yogurt, eggs, *spegepølse*, cheese, mango marmalade, and Cameroonian coffee, the perfect blend of Norwegian and Cameroonian cuisine.

After having eaten our fill, we set off for the Sunday's service. Dag drove very fast on the main thoroughfare going north. On the sides of this well-paved road with no shoulders, men and women walked with their children, and I saw an accident in the making every time a small child let go of his mother's hand.

We finally stopped at the tiny village of Ganani Dina where Dag was invited to preach. The church was the size of my small chateau in Ngaoundéré. It lay surrounded by compounds of huts, and was made of mud brick walls and a corrugated iron roof. People had congregated outside, but as the honored guests we were immediately brought into the church where benches built up from mud bricks lined the aisle on both sides. We were shown to "comfortable" chairs next to the altar. Left to our own devices until the service started about forty-five minutes later, we were enchanted when the choir entered singing and dancing. A young girl was leading it and two six-year-old boys drummed away to their hearts' delight. Finally, a long while later, the congregation entered. Facing the audience, Hans and I felt very much like animals on display, but this feeling was mitigated by the many luminous smiles sent our way by old men and bright-eyed children, the latter quiet as mice.

Dag's French "sermon"—whose topic I no longer remember—was translated to the Dii language by a young teacher and interestingly became a dialogue between the pastor and the congregation. Many comments and explications issued, from the older men especially, and the exchange was obviously entertaining, judging by the laughter that rippled through the church as the men stood bantering and telling their stories. This was followed by a long dedication ceremony for the elders, an offering, and communion, all combining to make it—at three hours—the longest service we had ever attended. Sore and stiff, we rose from the supposedly comfortable chairs while the congregation, having sat on backless mud benches the entire time, showed no such discomfort.

Outside, we were deluged with requests for medical advice, as we had been introduced in church as doctors. The requests were translated into French and we fielded them as best we could, apologizing that we had brought no medical equipment and were thus unable to examine anyone. We could have had a whole clinic there that day.

We were invited to the village chief's house for lunch. A fence of braided palm leaves surrounded his compound, which was very orderly, as the ground was swept daily. It had a number of huts made of mud bricks with grass roofs and no windows: a hut for the chief, one for each of his wives, and one for the children; a storage hut; a kitchen hut; and a hut for the chickens. Lunch was served in the children's hut, which was furnished with a bed and four lounge chairs. Sharing the meal with the local pastor, we were served corn couscous and a sauce of fish, green leaves, bouillon, and spices. Though it didn't contain very much fish, it was tasty. Washing our hands before the meal we ate with our fingers, no utensils being offered. Water was again passed after the meal to clean our sticky hands. Surprisingly, our host, the village chief, was absent and we did not meet him until after lunch. It appeared to be the custom that honored guests were served in seclusion. The impression it made on us to receive this meal, the best the village chief could afford, was hard to shake as we returned to the expansive house of the young Norwegian couple. By African standards they lived in luxury.

I knew I lived a very simple life in Cameroon, at least by American standards, yet I could not begin to understand the impression of wealth that I generated. It was clear from my interactions with Cameroonians, especially those who were unemployed — the majority — that they looked upon me as a millionaire. Students regularly stopped by my door wanting me to pay their tuition for the year. Families stopped to ask me for the sum needed to build them a house, and so it went. While I turned down all these early requests, Hans and I would later pay tuition for a number of young girls with whom we had become familiar. Yet, the sums requested in 1997 were so large, even by American standards, that I came to realize that because of the way I and other expatriates lived, and because of the fact that we had been able to afford to travel to Africa, we could only be viewed as sources of unending wealth.

I gave away small sums of money when I was first in Ngaoundéré, and it became a difficult issue. I thought I was unobtrusive about it, paying for patients who were unable to pay for their care. But news soon spread of my generosity and patients began pleading extreme poverty. This was an untenable situation and I subsequently decided I could no longer pay for anyone.

This was the state of mind I was in the day I was stopped by a young Liberian. As an Anglophone, unable to communicate in French, he hoped I spoke English. He said he was seeking care for his sick uncle. The two of them had no money, but had refugee papers entitling them to care; yet no one would help them. I went with him to the nurses, who said they could do nothing as long as they had no money. I found that particularly cruel, considering their status. For some reason, this young man touched me. Could it be because he expressed himself so well in English?

"Maybe you should take him to administration," the nurses said.

Brigitte, the Belgian secretary, told me there was indeed a charity fund, though it had little money in it. Because of the daily burden of dealing with patients' poverty, I was more than happy to turn the refugee over to someone else. I thanked her and left him there. I tried to tell myself that he was no longer my problem, that someone was taking care of him now and I needn't be concerned about him anymore. Yet still I worried. So why hadn't I helped him? Because I had gone on the defensive, thinking, "I am handing out money every day, I can't help them all, I am not a millionaire. There has to be a limit." But that made me feel no better. I couldn't get him out of my mind.

The next day I met him again and stopped to talk to him. He seemed content and said they had gotten medical help and that his uncle was feeling better. However, while the uncle had slept on a bench outside the hospital the night before, someone had stolen the shoes off his feet. They hadn't known what to do; the uncle needed his shoes since they were basically nomads. But then a kind doctor and his wife had given the uncle a pair of sandals. I will never forget the joy this act of kindness had brought to the young man. Such a simple act: giving away a pair of sandals.

I felt happy for him, yet I would continue to struggle over how to reconcile helping in a meaningful way without making people dependent. My thoughts went to Mother Teresa in India: she served people, the very poor and the sick. She did not dole out money, but recruited people from the West to work in her institutions and to take care of the poor and sick. There are many ways to help, and the best way is to help people become self-sufficient, not an entirely easy task, as I would later learn.

32. Benoît

Eventually my days settled into a more relaxed, though still challenging routine, and this was in no small part due to the nurse in the well-child clinic, Madame Frida, and to the head-nurse in maternity, Benoît. I had grown to respect and like Benoît. Granted, he was a distinctly odd man. He had become the head nurse in the maternity ward ten days before I arrived in Ngaoundéré. At that time he was in his early fifties and had been a nurse for thirty years, educated at the nursing school that used to belong to the hospital. He was a man of medium height, with coarse features, a broad smile and a loud, hearty laugh. He also had a forceful personality that brought him into frequent trouble. He had spent most of his career working in outlying clinics. His experience was vast and he was confident — in fact a little too confident — in his knowledge.

He ran his department with an iron fist. He had an overblown ego, often referring to himself in the third person, but he was scrupulously honest, and when he was once accused of stealing money, he beat his breast proclaiming, "No, Benoît does not do things like that. Never, never," he said, slicing the air. "Benoît is an honest person." Tirades like that made me think he protested too much, but I tended to believe him, as he was renowned for his honesty.

One of the joys when making rounds in maternity was seeing many babies doing well: the full-term babies who latched on to mother's breast immediately after birth and thrived during the mother's stay in maternity. And the few pre-term babies — the bread and butter of a busy Neonatal Intensive Care Unit in the U.S. — who, against all odds, continued to survive here.

Among the latter was a set of twin girls, born after the mother had gone into preterm labor at thirty weeks. Salwa was small-for-gestational age and weighed only two pounds three ounces. She was vigorous, however, and almost from the beginning she accepted mother's milk by gavage. Her weight dropped insignificantly after birth as is common in small-for-gestational age babies, but then she was slow to gain and we often despaired at her lack of progress and feared she wouldn't make it. I had none of the options I had at home that would have allowed me to increase her caloric intake; breast milk was it, and the amounts she was fed were limited to what she could tolerate. The mother, however, was ever-optimistic and was the driving force behind the babies' survival. She was meticulous about expressing breast milk for Salwa every two to three hours, and continued this far beyond the time when Fadwa, the other twin, was breast feeding well.

It was a joy to see this family because the father was also involved, always present at the mother's bedside. Keeping mother and child in the hospital was not an added burden to the family, as the hospital charged a one-time fee only for the bed. Thereafter patients could stay as long as needed without paying more. Eventually, Salwa too was breastfeeding and when she weighed three-and-a-half pounds, the parents insisted on taking her home. They brought the girls back for checkups and they continued to do fine.

As I was not an obstetrician, I could make few recommendations for treatment of the obstetric patients except to raise questions. Regularly we had a mother with pre-eclampsia. She was admitted to a small room without windows, where the light was always turned off, known as "the dark room." Decreased lighting was part of the regimen of treating pre-eclampsia and eclampsia, along with bedrest, magnesium sulphate, and antihypertensives.

I wondered if this total darkness approximated neglect, however, since there was an overemphasis on not disturbing the patient. I discussed this with Benoît, but he dismissed my concerns and reiterated that total darkness was imperative. Personally, I thought it extreme punishment. But I failed to realize that women in African villages often spend twelve hours of the day in total darkness, especially if the family has no kerosene lamps. Years later, as I sat with Cameroonian friends one evening, they began telling stories. As I listened, it became evident that each and every one of my friends knew different versions of the same story and they all knew the punchlines. These were stories told during the long evenings of darkness in the village. Maybe the pre-eclamptic woman in the dark room felt comfortable in this environment and her attendants might have regaled her with oft-told tales.

Benoît and I were making rounds in maternity one day when we were called to the delivery rooms. The nurses were quite disturbed by a baby who had just been born. Benoît took one look at the child and said tentatively, "Two heads?" He looked at me—gauging my face for my reaction –and then he laughed, "Of course not…but what is it?"

I turned the baby on its side and saw a sac the size of the baby's head located at the nape of the neck. The sac was soft, not covered by skin, but by a semi-translucent membrane. It tapered to a two-inch bridge that connected it to the occipital portion of the skull.

I explained it was an encephalocoele, a bulging of the membranes of the brain filled with cerebral fluid. What I couldn't determine was whether or not there was brain tissue in it.

"The parents won't like this," Benoît said. "They won't take care of the baby." He had said this of other babies, and I envisioned this child being put out for the lions to eat, except there was no wildlife of any sort around Ngaoundéré. It had all been hunted to extinction or driven out by the forward march of civilization. But—Benoît said—the parents likely wouldn't feed the baby.

"We need to examine this further," I said. "If there is no brain tissue in it, the sac can be removed with impunity. If there is brain tissue present, there could be neurologic consequences, though most often it's just scrambled brain tissue with no function. However, if we do nothing, the sac will get infected as will the brain, leading to the demise of the baby."

So basically we had two choices: do nothing and the baby would die, either through starvation or infection. Do something and the baby might survive. What the quality of life would be was uncertain, depending on the presence of other anomalies in the brain. I could not accept doing nothing, so we carefully dressed the encephalocoele with sterile wet dressings to ward off infection and to prevent the sac from drying up.

We had neither CT scan nor ultrasound, and x-ray would be of little help. I needed to be inventive, so I did the simplest thing, what Rod and I had done in the NICU in Duluth: I took the baby to the dark room. To the puzzlement of the eclamptic patient there, I put my mighty Maglite to the uncovered sac to transilluminate the encephalocoele and found nothing to suggest brain tissue, only fluid.

So now what? We had no neurosurgeon. I wasn't even sure, and nobody was, that there was a neurosurgeon in Cameroon. If there was one, he would have to be at the medical school in the capital and getting the child there was impossible.

I suggested to Benoît that we should have Dr. Yadji operate on the baby.

"Dr. Yadji?" It was clear he wasn't impressed by my suggestion. Dr. Yadji was a general surgeon of dubious qualifications. He claimed he had spent eight years in training as a surgeon at the university hospital in Yaoundé, but no one had ever seen any documentation of that nor had he demonstrated incontrovertible capabilities. I wasn't too happy either with the idea, but it was the child's only chance. As long as sterile procedure was observed Dr. Yadji should be able to tie off the stalk that attached the sac to the brain, and then close the skin over it.

I approached Dr. Yadji, a short, thin man who rarely smiled and who always seemed full of himself, and asked him to see the baby. I told him what he should be able to do. He seemed flattered that I entrusted this infant to him, that I thought he could do a neurosurgical procedure, and he agreed to do it. By this time, the parents had seen the baby. We told them of the proposed surgery and they gave us the green light to go ahead.

Dr. Yadji took the child to surgery. The procedure was tolerated well and the baby was returned to the maternity ward in good condition. He looked quite normal now and the parents were immensely pleased. But while the parents weren't looking, Benoît pointed to the suture line with great disapproval.

"Ay-yah-yah," he said.

Dr. Yadji's suturing was like nothing I had ever seen. A puckered mouth with the edges approximated so unevenly that the skin buckled into huge bulges, sewn together with thick black silk sutures.

Benoît and I watched the baby's recovery with concern. The incision healed well, however, without infection. The baby fed at his mother's breast with enthusiasm. The postoperative course was uneventful. I could find no neurologic abnormalities or deficits in the baby, though that did not exclude that such might be found in the future.

Benoît went around shaking his head. He could not believe the outcome of this patient, but he was immensely proud of "our" accomplishments. We discharged the baby, and though we asked that he be brought back, I never saw him again.

This was of concern, because despite the pleasure the parents had shown after the child had surgery, they might still consider him a defective child. Certainly with an ugly scar at the back of his head he did not look like other children. As with the child with Trisomy 13/18 that I had diagnosed earlier, this was not a matter of teaching parents how to care for their handicapped child. There was much more at stake. First of all the parents would have to accept their child as he was. In Africa, more than anywhere else, people with handicaps, whether acquired at birth or after birth, are seen as less than human. The parents are ashamed of the child and usually hide the child away. According to tradition, disability is a curse caused by terrible wrongdoing, either on the part of the parents or other family members, and is seen as a punishment from a deity. It can also be viewed as a spell cast by someone wishing the family harm. In rural communities the disabled child can be feared like an evil spirit, is often isolated in the house, has lowest priority when it comes to who is fed, is unloved, and is often abused. This is a sad state of affairs since in Africa children are so much more at risk of becoming disabled from difficult births, accidents, war, and diseases caused by, for example, lack of vaccinations or delayed treatment of malaria, than children in developed nations. Often these disabled children are not thought worthy of an education, and if they are sent to school, they must deal with discrimination, bullying, and handicap-inaccessible school buildings. It is an issue that some institutions have started to address, but what is needed is an attitude change among the general population, which will be a very gradual process.

Of course the attitude toward children with handicaps is also a pragmatic one. Resources are limited and it seems reasonable that families should ask why they should share their meager resources with a child who will never grow up to become a useful family member. Feeding a handicapped child may mean that their normal and potentially productive children, the ones that will support the parents in old age, may starve.

It is very hard to reconcile this attitude with the West's attitude toward sick, dying, or defective newborns. I thought of the baby in Duluth who was born without a brain, and how the parents grieved the loss of the normal baby they had anticipated, yet accepted and loved her as she was. Parents of the child Benoît and I were dealing with showed no signs of grieving.

Western society is one of surpluses, including a surplus of emotional energy. We have been conditioned to having such high expectations for pregnancy that we expect the perfect child. When that is not delivered, we allow ourselves the luxury of grieving deeply. Does our life of relative extravagance compared to that of many in this world make us feel entitled to a life without mishaps? Does our standard of living relieve us of the immediate concerns for survival experienced by another age or by people of developing nations, to the extent that we have surplus energy to grieve? There were many questions to ponder.

Later that day a father and mother arrived on a motorcycle taxi with a one-year-old in their arms. They walked into my office, laid the child on my table, and unwrapped the blankets. As I leaned over with my stethoscope to listen to the baby, my hand grazed cold skin. The child, unbeknownst to the parents, had already died. Within minutes they realized and accepted that, wrapped her up again, and stoically and without shedding a tear, walked out. It was hard to believe they felt no emotion, but they were unable to let their emotions be tied up in grieving. There were more immediate concerns, such as daily survival. Death was always with them and they had few expectations for life. Their child was important while alive, but not in death.

I found it difficult to get used to this culture's attitude toward defective children, let alone its ready acceptance of death, especially the death of newborns. I often felt my efforts to save a baby were counter to the wishes of staff and family, and at times a dead newborn was given little respect: he was buried in the backyard without a gravestone to mark his grave. It was as if the child were not considered a real person. That we in Western society should have enough energy to grieve our losses is healing, and I felt sad that no one seemed to grieve the loss of a newborn.

While I was in Ngaoundéré a well-known community member died. The wake lasted for a week and people grieved, sometimes loudly. He would have an elaborate gravesite. It seemed to me that in Africa one grieved for the loss of an ancestor, for the past, but not for the loss of a future—and all that a baby has is its future. Working with Benoît helped me gain some insight into these cultural differences, though I would later better understand why mothers feared loving a baby they might so easily lose.

So my worry for this child with the encephalocele was well founded. He lived in a remote village and we had no social worker or public health nurse who could check on his welfare.

One day I saw a different and less gentle side of Benoît's personality. As I was leaving maternity I saw a huge altercation by the entrance to the ward. Benoît was walking around shouting, apparently infuriated by a family. When I asked what was going on, he just said, "They don't want to pay for the patient," pointing to the family of a woman who had had a Caesarian section, "but this is none of your concern."

He had no time for people who wouldn't (couldn't) pay for their care. If a woman had a Caesarian section and didn't pay, he held her hostage until the family paid. Some would say that this was counterproductive and cruel, but maybe he knew the family and knew that they indeed *could* pay. I later learned that this was common practice in former mission hospitals. Patients' families would try everything in their power to avoid paying. This was a problem for the hospital and was one of the causes of its insolvency. Years later, at a church hospital in western Cameroon I saw a house that was simply a prison where patients were held hostage until someone paid for their care.

Thus, I recognized that Benoît was a complicated man who needed to be seen in the African context. When he made rounds seeing the patients, he was compassionate and caring, understanding of the women's problems, working with them in a paternalistic way. One example was a patient I saw one of the first days I rounded with him. The patient was a sixteen-year-old Muslim girl who had become pregnant out of wedlock; in view of the frequency of rape of young girls, she may well have been a victim of rape, yet her father had been furious and had disowned her. The baby had died at birth and the girl had developed a puerperal infection that needed treatment. Benoît had interceded for the girl with her father and had convinced him to pay for the girl's treatment. So Benoît had indeed acted in a very paternal way toward this girl. She immediately got better after two doses of ampicillin and the father decided he wasn't going to pay for more and took her home. He may not have thought she was worth spending any more money on, but at least he accepted her back into his house again.

Though Benoît at first had stated, "in Africa we don't put IVs in babies," he quickly decided that he was willing to learn to do so and placed almost all subsequent IVs. He assimilated everything I taught him, and if his ego had not gotten in the way and he had stayed, maybe it would have taken less time to get appropriate infant care in maternity at Ngaoundéré Protestant Hospital.

He had come to Ngaoundéré from the provincial town of Meiganga where he had been head of an integrated health clinic, one among the many belonging to the Evangelical Lutheran Church of Cameroon. He was removed from there when a lawsuit was filed against him (and the church) for wrongful death of a woman who keeled over outside his clinic and died. As it happened, she had not been seen at the clinic, so he was not responsible and was acquitted. Yet the powers that be (or were) decided he would be better off in Ngaoundéré.

Later, at the end of my stay in 1997, he got into a controversy with the general surgeon, Dr. Yadji, about the appropriate treatment of pregnancy-induced hypertension. He stubbornly adhered to what he had learned as a young nurse and belittled Dr. Yadji's opinion. Somehow the nursing supervisor became involved in this as well and the church decided to move all three rabble-rousers as far from each other as possible. Thus Benoît ended up running a clinic in Bankim to the southwest of Ngaoundéré for the rest of his career.

With the surprising development of St. Mary's/Duluth Clinic (later Essentia Health East), at Hans's and my instigation, entering into a partnership with the Protestant Hospital at Ngaoundéré, and as we began our educational exchange program with the hospital, we saw Benoît as a candidate to bring to Duluth, but his employer, the Cameroonian Lutheran Church, refused to send him. He was a troublemaker who didn't merit this honor. As a consequence of this and many other experiences, Benoît came to see himself as a victim: everyone was out to get him. That he himself might have contributed to this state of things was beyond his imagination.

Benoît was a hard worker throughout his career, supplementing his income by doing upholstering. He put one daughter, Elizabeth, a very beautiful and gracious woman, through medical school. She later became an ophthalmologist and a good friend of ours and for a number of years she ran Ngaoundéré Hospital's eye clinic. Another daughter, Natalie, he put through pharmacy school. A third daughter became an engineer. His three sons were less ambitious. Judging by his family, he is a model Cameroonian citizen, though not necessarily credited as such by his coworkers. His wife is a gracious, but very retiring person who is also a nurse, and whom we know much less well. Hans and I have maintained a strong friendship with Benoît, and every time we meet he regales us with stories of his family and with what is going on in his life.

33. Garoua-Boulaï

A charming young man with dreadlocks stood at our door. It was early evening. Lightning flashed across the dark sky followed by crashing thunderbolts. Rain lashed at the guy, who was soaked through. We asked him in.

"I'm married to Debbie, the American nurse in Garoua-Boulaï," he said. "I have come to Ngaoundéré on an errand and am going back to G.-B. tomorrow. Debbie tells me you are supposed to go with me."

In the middle of July our daughter, Christine, had joined me. She had finished the first year of her RN/NP degree program at the University of Pennsylvania, and had worked with me for about a week at Ngaoundéré hospital. This young man's visit came as a surprise to us. Though Christine and I had informally consented to spend some time at one of the other two hospitals of the Cameroonian Lutheran Church, we had had no warning of when. In fluent English and with an American accent, the young man said, "My name is David [Da'veed, he pronounced it]. You should have gotten a message that I was coming to pick you up."

In 1997 the only contact between mission stations was by radio. Usually there was communication every morning at seven, but since Jim and Karen Noss had gone home on leave, the communication system had broken down.

"I guess the message wasn't relayed," I said.

"Will you be able to go with me tomorrow?" he asked.

Christine and I looked at each other. Though hesitant we quickly decided that we could probably get ready.

We both liked to plan things well in advance. We had to think this through. What did we need to do to get ready?

"I just want you to know the trip will be long," David said, "it's only one hundred thirty-five kilometers (about eighty-five miles), but it will probably take six or seven hours."

We told him we would be ready to go the next morning at eight. We started packing that same evening. We knew the roads were bad; if the car broke down or there were mishaps, we would need sustenance, and we planned accordingly. Unlike in the U.S., there were no convenience stores along the way. We had three half-gallon bottles of filtered water in the refrigerator, as well as pineapple and papaya that we cut up and put in a plastic container. In the morning Christine would go to the small market outside the gates to buy several fresh baked baguettes, one of the benefits of the French legacy. We had cheese to go with the bread. We would be all set.

At around 8:30 the next morning, David came by in a Toyota truck with a covered load. It seemed there was plenty of space in the extended cab for the three of us. However, while still in town, David made several stops and before we knew it we were four women crammed into the back seat—we could barely breathe—and three men in front. It appeared that rumor about our departure had spread, and people wanting to visit family were hitching a ride. So much for relaxed travel!

The route to Garoua-Boulaï was on a poorly maintained dirt road. The heavy rains had cut deep ruts into it and large trucks hauling goods had exacerbated the potholes into small ponds. Maybe it was a good thing that we were seated so closely. We bolstered each other as we continuously were thrown from side to side while David tried to avoid the worst holes. Progress was slow.

When we were about an hour out of Ngaoundéré, we felt the car slowly sliding on the very slippery, wet clay road…there was no stopping it…and soon we found ourselves in the ditch with the car tilting at a forty-five degree angle. David turned off the engine and sat there thinking for a while. Then he turned on the engine, again putting it in gear. Nothing happened. I was sitting on the high end of the seat, grabbing hold of the overhead handle so as not to completely squash Christine and the two other women in the back seat. This was what we had feared: an accident stranding us. Few cars were on the road and there was no immediate help at hand. We could not get out of the car, at least not unless someone came along who was able, from the outside, to pull open the doors that were lying on top of David and me on the driver's side of the car. But before anyone came along, David decided to give it another try. He started up the engine again, and very slowly—by some miracle—we began to move forward at an angle...he got traction...we held our breath...the car righted itself and...hallelujah, we were back on the road.

We continued on our way at a maddeningly slow pace, sometimes driving into the bush to circumvent the enormous craters in the road. We shuddered whenever we saw a big, top-heavy truck coming toward us, and repeatedly this scenario was played out: the truck approached a huge pothole...and...tilted. Would it topple and crush us? Would its load come tumbling down on us? But we managed to escape disaster every time.

As we got closer to our destination, our co-travelers were let off at villages along the way. By the time we reached Garoua-Boulaï there was only David, Christine and me left.

Here we found an even prettier campus than in Ngaoundéré, with fewer houses and more trees. We were installed in a spacious two-bedroom guesthouse and were invited for dinner by the house parents of the American boarding school for missionary children, Cathy and John Larson. Cathy was outgoing and talkative as she prepared dinner. She and John had come here some years before on a visit with a church group. They saw the need for their services and signed up for a five-year stint. They loved being house parents. They had only about seven kids at the present time. She also told us that the school had a swimming pool that we could use.

The next day, we got busy seeing patients in the outpatient clinic and in the hospital. Christine, as a nursing student, helped with practical things like setting up IVs and changing dressings. On the first day we saw a ten-month old child with AIDS whose mother had died from the disease. The child was severely malnourished, partly because of the AIDS, partly because he had received no mother's milk. He was already too far gone and there was nothing we could do for him. Two days later he was dead.

The missionary physician from Madagascar, Dr. Heuric, was a capable surgeon, and when a ten-year-old boy was brought in with what on x-ray looked like ileus, we opened up his belly, suspecting a mechanical obstruction. His peritoneum, however, was peppered with white spots: the granulomas of miliary tuberculosis, which were causing a functional obstruction. We closed him up and started him on streptomycin. After less than a week, he was somewhat better and was beginning to have bowel sounds, but he was very emaciated and ate little. Intravenous nutrition would have been desirable, but not feasible here. We wanted to give him a continuous duodenal drip of a high-calorie formula that we asked a former missionary nurse, Lorraine Haugen, to concoct so he could gain weight. In retirement, Lorraine had returned to Cameroon as a volunteer and every day she made a large amount of nutritious porridge that she fed to malnourished children who came to the hospital compound from the village, paying for it out of her own pocket. Sure, she said, she could make a nutritious drip for our patient. Several other children had both malaria and typhus with high fevers, rashes, and delirium. We treated them with a quinine derivative and chloramphenicol.

I saw a twelve-year-old boy in the clinic with a large mass on one cheek. He was an orphan, and an uncle brought him from the neighboring country of CAR (the Central African Republic). He had Burkitt's lymphoma, a disease I had read about, but had never encountered. It is endemic in equatorial Africa and is common in children with chronic malaria, which makes them less resistant to the Epstein-Barr virus, the cause of the lymphoma. The uncle said that the tumor had grown very rapidly from a small plum-sized growth to its present grapefruit size. I found the pharmacy had endoxan, a European preparation of cyclophosphamide, which is effective in this disease. I hospitalized the child, a quiet, somewhat chubby young boy, and started him on the medication. The uncle was very solicitous toward the child and paid willingly for the oral medication. Despite his apparent chubbiness the boy was malnourished. His belly was distended, he was edematous, and had the "wet" form of malnutrition: protein malnutrition or *Kwashiorkor*. I emphasized good nutrition and here we had the prerogative of actually providing better nutrition to patients with Lorraine's porridge. I talked to the uncle at length about the importance of finishing the treatment regime.

Within days I was gratified to see the tumor diminish rapidly. The boy appeared somewhat perkier and I was looking forward to a full recovery.

However, on rounds one week later, I found there was no one in the boy's bed. I asked the nurses if they had transferred him to another room. No, they hadn't. The uncle had become increasingly antsy during the last couple of days, they said. He wanted to leave, claiming he had urgent things to take care of at home. Why had no one told me? I had contemplated sending the child home with medication, but was wary of doing so. With the tumor shrinking so rapidly there could be complications. By the end of the day, since we had been unable to find the child in the hospital, we assumed the uncle had left with him, but without the medication.

By this time I had become somewhat immune to the scenario of patients leaving before the end of their treatment. They could leave at will, I had no power to keep them, but I didn't always comprehend their motivations. The lack of understanding of the seriousness of the illness and the lack of money were contributing factors, but there could be others, including fear of sorcery. Had the uncle suspected I was trying to poison the child? Had a medicine man offered cheaper treatment? Those were all unspoken issues that I was aware of, but with which I had no experience.

One of the customs I sometimes could get no explanation for was the ritual of scarification, the cutting into skin with the purpose of creating scars. They could be done for aesthetic, religious, or social reasons, but sometimes the reason wasn't clear. I encountered a less than one-year-old child in the hospital with cuts on the soles of his feet that had become infected. He was febrile and in great pain, both his feet pitifully swollen and oozing with infection. I didn't know why the ritual had been employed. Was it to cast out evil spirits? Surely they were not for tribal identity reasons when placed under the feet. Fortunately I was able to treat the boy with IV antibiotics. His fever subsided, the swelling went down, and his wounds healed quickly. But I anticipated that the boy would forever have painful feet from the scars this practice left.

In Ngaoundéré I had encountered a five-year-old girl the parents had brought in with eye lesions. The child's eyes had been inflamed and red a month before, and her parents had brought her to the local witch doctor, who treated her eyes with a solution of some sort. The eyes had at first become even more inflamed. The witch doctor told the parents she would get better, but the results were devastating. Both eyes were now completely cloudy and she had lost her vision. The parents wondered what I could do about it. I felt sick at heart and sat staring at her in silence for a long time, while anger ran through me. I wanted to ask the parents, "How could you have let the witch doctor do this to your child?

This is child abuse. How could you?" But of course, it wasn't child abuse; it was ignorance. They probably truly thought they were doing the best for their child. But there also was no doubt that they were destroyed by the results. They must have had some hope that I could fix her eyes or they wouldn't have brought her to me. I had her see the eye doctor who agreed with me that this was irreversible. Deep down, they must have known this would be the answer, because they didn't react, they just got up and left, taking the girl with them. How many blows can you take in a lifetime? It seemed my patients' families were shouldering one blow after another and just accepting them because they were an inevitable part of life—and for them they were.

While in Ngaoundéré, Christine and I had communicated with home mainly via fax. Occasionally we had actually been able to call the U.S. on the phone. In Garoua-Boulaï we were totally *incommunicado,* no telephone, no fax. There was regular mail, which was so slow, however, that it made no sense for transients like us to use it. We would be back home before the mail arrived. There was something strangely liberating about being out of reach—at least for a brief time. We spent our free time reading and going for walks in the countryside—feeling quite the Victorians.

In the surroundings of the mission station, the grass was above our heads. In between were fields of cassava and groundnuts. We followed paths, not knowing for sure where they would take us. Snakes—among them the poisonous green mamba—occupy these grasslands; we fortunately never encountered any. But one day we got lost and accidentally strayed across the border to the Central African Republic. Crossing any international border without passports, and at any place other than regular checkpoints, is illegal. Fortunately, we happened upon friendly Cameroonian border guards who quickly got us back on track. I now think of the three young people who a few years ago strayed across the border from Iraq into Iran only to be arrested and jailed. We felt lucky—being jailed in the Central African Republic, or in Cameroon for that matter, could be deadly—and we headed back to the compound and the pool to cool off.

When at the apartment again, we moved chairs onto the porch and relaxed with a glass of wine, quite the civilized thing to do. The weather was gorgeous, just warm and not hot this late in the day. Green lawns with luscious mango trees stretched out in front of us, and all we could hear were the birds. Then suddenly the orchestral tones of Debussy's *L'après-midi d'un faun* drifted across to our porch from Lorraine's apartment next door. It felt like a little bit of heaven.

Our days in Garoua-Boulaï ended and we hitched a ride with a missionary to Meiganga. There we stayed in one of the guesthouses for a couple of nights before traveling back to Ngaoundéré with Tom and Sharyn Christensen. Tom was a professor at the Lutheran Seminary in Meiganga.

At dinner that first night with Tom and Sharyn, we learned about the person who had recently stayed in the guesthouse we were in. She was a young Norwegian missionary from Poli, in the north of Cameroon, who had come here on vacation. Three Cameroonians had followed her here. They had broken into her guesthouse, abducted her in a pickup truck, and brought her into the bush. After repeatedly raping her they had thrown her body from the car. She was found there by villagers and brought back to Meiganga. She recovered, and though severely traumatized, vowed to come back to Cameroon.

Needless to say this information did not comfort us and we were a little on edge when Christine that evening heard someone on the porch of the guesthouse. Fortunately—or unfortunately—all it turned out to be was a guard, the one who was supposed to protect us, fast asleep on the ground.

34. The Bible Translator

He stopped by the *chateau* where I was reading on the back stoop to the kitchen while keeping an eye on mulberries I was cooking to make juice. This was early in my stay in Ngaoundéré.

"Have a look at this," he said, throwing his shirt over his head, exposing his old white man's back. "How do you like those things?"

The lower part of his back had clusters of large, angry red boils. I wasn't quite sure what his intent was in showing them to me. Was he going to ask me for help? Preempting him, I said, "What are you going to do about them?"

"Oh, nothing."

"Why?"

"They'll go away. I've had them before."

"How did you get them?"

"Well," he said, "you may have noticed the excess of rotten mango fruits under the trees. They are abuzz with mango flies that have a preference for laying their eggs in something wet, like my laundry on the line. Once those shirts are dry and I wear them, the eggs are in a nice, snug, and warm spot where they develop into larvae that burrow into my back. When the boils get bigger, you squeeze out the larvae and the boils disappear. Right now I am just a host for them."

"I guess I wouldn't hang my shirts outside if I were you."

"Well, if only I had ironed them, I would have killed the eggs, but I didn't, so I guess I'll have to live with it," he said with a smile. From then on I hung all my laundry inside to dry.

Ed Mueller was my neighbor on one side. I had already learned there were many odd white people hanging about in Africa. I had first met him when he came to my door suggesting I employ a young Cameroonian woman, Elisabet, as my cook-cleaner. I took her on to give her a job, though, frankly, I thought I could manage cooking my own meals and cleaning my very small house by myself. She turned out to be one of many people Ed felt needed his help. Elisabet's husband had discarded her because she was unable to bear children. Sexually transmitted diseases are the most common cause of infertility in Africa and likely the cause of hers. Yet she had a child to care for. A brother had more mouths to feed than he could afford, so he gave her one of his daughters, a four-year-old, to rear. I was glad to be able to help this young woman—her salary was all of twenty dollars per month—and was delighted by her child.

Ed's house was usually filled with young Cameroonians who ate most of his food and also borrowed the cushions off his chairs, never returning them, so that now he had nowhere to sit.

He had come to Africa as a Bible translator many years before, and with his wife he had lived in Balkossa, in the remote far west of Cameroon. She wrote primers in Chamba, the tribal language, and taught people to read, while Ed worked on translating the New Testament into the same language. He had set up solar panels in the village to produce the electricity to run his computers and printers. But eventually his collaborators got fed up: his wife left him and his translators wanted to go to the city. Besides, there were too many people there who wanted something from him, he said. So now he worked out of Ngaoundéré, ignoring the fact that here, people also plundered him.

One day, shortly after we had returned from Garoua-Boulaï and just before we left to return to the United States, Ed invited Christine and me to go with him and Tom and Sharyn Christensen to a fish restaurant. Tom and Sharyn drove there separately, and Ed took Christine and me in his Toyota van. Between the front seats was a can of gasoline. I wondered aloud why he carried gas inside his car. Ed said that the fuel pump was broken, so he had replaced it with this can, from which the gasoline flowed passively to the engine.

"It works quite well," he said, marveling at his own ingenuity. The car smelled of gas, however, and though he kept the windows open, I worried about riding in his car. A cigarette butt thrown into it from the outside could blow us all up; fortunately few Cameroonians smoke, so that may not have been likely. Christine and I chose to sit in the back, away from the gas can, a good idea, it seemed, until I realized I couldn't open the back door from the inside.

The streets leading to the fish restaurant were unpaved and slippery after the rains. The car tipped from one side to another, spilling gasoline, as we traversed large depressions in the road. A five-by-five-foot rock sat in the middle of one street and traffic must have been forced to pass around it from time immemorial. It was after dark, there were no street-lights, and the lights of the van were faint. Eventually we stopped in a busy street lined by many small restaurants, one-story mud houses with tin roofs whose interior lights barely penetrated the gloom outside. From the car, Ed, Christine, and I made our way into the darkness, a flashlight lighting up a circle in front of us as we stepped over the deep, open gutters. It struck me that this was how medieval Europe must have looked.

We climbed onto the porch of a fish restaurant, where sat a woman tending a huge container of fish on ice, *capitaine*, an inland lake fish. Next to her was a large grill in which she was burning wood. She encouraged us to pick out the fish we wanted; she would bring it to us when it was done. The restaurant seemed like a private home with several rooms for guests. The doors, painted in garish colors were worn and dirty, as were the walls and tiny windows. The furniture, with dark upholstery that sheltered much dirt, consisted of large armchairs that fit no real person's body. Made locally and touted to be comfortable, they seemed intended for giants. The drinks offered were *pamplemousse,* a pineapple pop; *Djino*, a mixed fruit pop; and beer. I ordered a one-liter bottle of *trente-trois (33)*, a local beer, to share with Christine.

Soon our fish arrived, on individual plates with *pommes frites,* mayonnaise, and a very spicy sauce in which to dip the fish. Before that a pail of water, along with soap and a well-worn but clean towel, had been passed around so we could wash our hands. There were no utensils. After tasting just a few bites, I was convinced it was one of the tastiest meals I would ever have. The fish and sauce were delicious, the French-fries fantastic. That I had to eat with my fingers only added to the pleasure. Sharyn, Tom, Ed, Christine and I reminisced about other similar eating adventures while we shared our life stories.

As we sat back to relax after the meal, I shared with them an experience I had had that day. Looking out the windows while making rounds, I had seen a woman come walking across the parking lot toward maternity, stark naked. When she reached the steps she knelt, holding her hands together as if in prayer. Then she got up and seated herself on the bench outside the entrance. Employees, who congregated around her later, told me she was psychotic. Apparently she had lost a child in maternity and had gone mad. In view of the stoicism women generally display when their children die, this was surprising to me. I didn't know what happened to her afterwards. We discussed the painful lack of psychiatrists or psychiatric care in town—and in Cameroon in general—while concluding there really was no one to help her.

As we left the restaurant, Ed invited Tom, Sharyn, Christine, and me to a disco to "live it up," as he said. Tom and Sharyn declined and went back to the compound. Christine and I did not have any particular desire to visit a disco either and signaled each other with our eyes before we reluctantly said yes. The disco was close by. As we entered, it became obvious that many customers were prostitutes. Ed declared they were all his friends, and indeed they all seemed to know him. We didn't stay long, however. Neither the swirling lights nor the loud music attracted us, but we conceded that the disco lent Ngaoundéré a cosmopolitan air. We also concluded that Ed must spend a number of his evenings here, even though the place seemed to attract mostly young people and prostitutes. He was disappointed that we didn't want to "live it up." We assured him that it had been an experience we wouldn't have been without, and he reluctantly drove us home.

I marveled at the life Ed Mueller, then probably in his late sixties, led here in the deepest part of Africa. An expert in one of the 220 languages of Cameroon, he labored intensely with a couple of local translators to translate the Bible into Chamba. He worked for the Lutheran Bible Translators, an organization that operates in many countries around the world and whose vision it is to see the Bible accessible to all people in the language they understand best. We assumed Ed did an acceptable job, as we saw his supervisors fly in to check on his progress. Did he do this because he found it of paramount importance that the Bible be translated into all languages? Was it his Christian faith that compelled him to do this work? One had the feeling that somehow the faith had been lost along the way and that he had now become stuck in a lifestyle from which he didn't want to extricate himself. Ed was generous to a fault, giving away what he owned, and the people obviously loved him. Had he lost his purpose in life after his wife of thirty years left him? Or had he actually found it? He said he lived like the locals, except it seemed to us that the locals took advantage of him. He disagreed, saying he shared like the locals share, and maybe he knew the truth of that better than we did.

As we came back to the compound that evening, a full moon illuminated the ghostly grass and trees, making our flashlights obsolete. Two weeks earlier, I had noticed a half-moon in the sky. It lay flat on its back; in a position unlike anything I had seen in the northern hemisphere—perhaps mirroring the more relaxed attitude of the local population? As we arrived at the little knoll on which sat my house, we spotted the Southern Cross low in the sky. I would miss this equatorial view of the firmament.

Epilogue

Each man should frame life so that at some future hour fact and his dreaming meet.

Victor Hugo

I reached the end of my first stay in Cameroon in mid-August, 1997. Three months had not been enough time for me to get acclimated to working in a developing country, but I was ready to leave and unsure that I would ever return. It had been a challenging time. I longed to be back home.

When Hans had left, he had flown to Douala, where he would spend a day before getting on the plane for home. However, for some reason, his name on the passenger list on the Air France flight to Paris had disappeared, his travel plans became bungled, and he was stuck in Douala. He had gone back and forth to the Air France office every day to see if there was a seat for him on a plane, but was told it could be two weeks before he could get a flight out. He had been miserable and upset at having to spend extra days in that sweltering, dirty port city. He called to tell me how he hated it and assured me he would never come back to Cameroon. But I had underestimated him. While holed up at the *Ibis* Hotel waiting for a flight, he began thinking about how he and I could be instruments for change at Ngaoundéré Hospital. Hans is a visionary, and soon, instead of giving up on Ngaoundéré, he developed a plan for how we could make a difference there.

When learning about it upon my return to the U.S., I was unsure I wanted to have anything to do with it, but months went by and he did not to give up. How the tables had turned, I thought. Here was the guy who had opposed me going to Cameroon in the first place, and now he was hatching a plan for further commitment. In the end, he won me over, as he had known he would.

What he was proposing was an educational exchange involving Cameroonians coming to St. Mary's/Duluth Clinic (later Essentia Health East) to gain knowledge in a particular field, and nurses and other personnel from SMDC going to Cameroon to learn about the culture and teach their particular skills. I could see how the plan might have merit, and though I was loath to make a commitment, I collaborated with Hans in hatching out a plan.

The following year we presented a proposal to the SMDC Board requesting funding for the exchange and asking for permission to bring Cameroonians to SMDC for education. We were pleasantly surprised and grateful when the Board wholeheartedly endorsed the plan and granted funding for a three-year period.

This plan was then presented to the Board of the Cameroonian Lutheran Church, which was running the hospital. It was met with great skepticism. What was this unknown organization up to—one associated with a Catholic hospital to boot—making that kind of proposal? It was not until we had convinced the CEO of SMDC, Dr. Peter Person, and the Chairman of St. Mary's Hospital Board, Sister Kathleen Hofer, to go with us to Cameroon to have conversations with the leaders of the Cameroonian Lutheran Church that the proposal was accepted. Our church in Duluth, First Lutheran, would help sponsor the exchange students and serve as their host congregation during their stay in Duluth.

That same fall, two Cameroonians came to Duluth. We had not been free to choose the candidates. The Church looked at this opportunity as a way to give worthy employees a perk. What made them worthy wasn't always certain; it could be that they were of the same tribe as the president of the church or that he or some other person in a position of power owed them something. We had suggested Benoît, but that was out of the question. He was a rabble-rouser, they said, and besides he didn't belong to the right tribe. Other people were chosen.

This first exchange was as much a learning experience for us as for the Cameroonians. One of the Cameroonians, a doctor, was housed with a young family where the wife was a practicing physician and the husband a stay-at-home dad for their young children. This arrangement completely threw off the Cameroonian doctor. He was set in his ways. He had a brood of children and a wife who catered to all his needs. This household where the husband did the wife's job was something he had trouble accepting and he asked to be placed in another home.

Two nurses from SMDC next went to Cameroon that following spring. This was a success. Soon we had doctors and nurses going back and forth on a regular basis and the Cameroon Healthcare Development Program (CHDP) took off.

During the past fourteen years since the inception of the program, some twenty medical people from Duluth have worked in Cameroon and about fifteen medical or paramedical personnel from Cameroon have come to Duluth. Hans and I have returned yearly to Ngaoundéré for one to two months each time, treating patients there and supervising program developments and building projects. Early on, we realized a need for biomedical equipment and were able to acquire SMDC equipment that was in the process of being exchanged for newer and better technology. An emergency room was also needed. We found funding for that and sent a team to Cameroon to teach emergency care to the nurses. We procured funds for a kitchen for patients' families, and rotary clubs in Duluth and surrounding area paid for an ICU and a Burn Center. Other needs and projects announced themselves.

While we were in Cameroon in 2006 for the grand opening of the ICU and Burn Center, the director of the health system of the Cameroonian Lutheran Church, Dr. Daniel Salpou, gave me the task of building a neonatal unit in the existing OB department. We found money for it and Hans designed the unit with my help and the help of an American pediatrician and a Norwegian nurse, who both were working in Ngaoundéré at the time. We had walls torn down to accommodate the unit and it was ready by the time we left. This was something that I had long wanted to see. It would not be a neonatal *intensive* care unit since we could not offer intensive care, but it became a unit where preemies and sick newborns were cared for. Protocols for feedings, medications, and cares were set up. The result has been a decrease in infant mortality, and especially in the mortality of preemies.

Was the work in Cameroon the goal I had waited all my professional life to achieve? Was this what it was all about when at fourteen I had decided to become a doctor? Maybe in some sense it was. I wanted to make a difference by caring for the sick and poor, nothing more specific, and I ended up caring for the most vulnerable of patients, babies whom previous generations had been unable to care for, and whom few developing cultures were ready to give a chance. I wasn't predestined to become a neonatologist. I could just as easily have become a psychiatrist, my first choice when my brother was diagnosed with schizophrenia. I could also have become a surgeon, a notion I briefly entertained when I was an intern. However, pediatrics called, and neonatology drew me in, and I have never regretted my professional path.

I have lived my life out on four continents. On three of them I was a stranger, and even in my native country I was often viewed as different. I grew up in a working class neighborhood in Aarhus, but I was not working class, even though we were poor. My father had come from a highly educated family and we felt we had roots in the intelligentsia of the country. However, though my siblings and I attended The Latin School in Aarhus for students destined for a higher education, I was the only one in my generation—and the first woman in all generations of my family—to go to university.

As I think back on the stories in this book, it is evident that the reason many of the stories have stayed with me is because of their subtexts: the "firsts"—*first* woman physician, *first* transport, and *first* ventilator patient—and the culturally different, the outsiders, the ones who are viewed as and who feel themselves as not being part of the mainstream: the family of the Cree baby from Canada, Jimmy, and Forest Breeze with his hippie parents. I also vividly remember the abused and those who were hurt by random acts of destruction: the abused twins, Jason, who stood to lose not only a leg but a life, and the father whose wife and son met their deaths in one tragic collision. The "less than human" children with severe congenital malformations—Erik with heart disease, Grace with no brain, the children in Cameroon with trisomy 13/18 and encephalocoele, and others, whose stories I have not told—will always be remembered. These were the outsiders, the ones who were different *and* special, in a way. They have stayed with me because they were some of my greatest challenges yet also the ones that urged me on.

At so many points in my life I have chosen "the different", "the road less traveled." That I have "traveled" at all, and in a fairly straight line is in large part due to Hans, my husband and partner, who has kept me anchored. I might have become lost if it weren't for him. Yet, despite the detours, I have ended up where I began: I have made it full circle back to the developing world. Though I, in 1996, had misgivings about being able to practice neonatology in Cameroon, by 2006, I knew that something was changing in the care of newborns there, especially at Ngaoundéré Protestant Hospital. My call to go to Cameroon led to hope for many children—hope for life and hope for a future. Hope has permeated my working life: the hope and love I learned from the parents of my babies. In uncertainty, hope is what sustains you.

In that life Hans was with me all the way and he helped shape it in so many respects. What a gift that life has been!

About the Author

Dr. Martha A. Aas lives in Duluth, Minnesota. She was born in Denmark where she went to medical school. She was a neonatologist at St. Mary's Medical Center/Duluth Clinic for twenty-three years and, with her husband, she has directed the Cameroon Healthcare Development Program for the past fourteen years. She is the author of the memoir *Pearls on a String.*

ACKNOWLEDGMENTS

Thanks go to my fellow writers at Lake Superior Memoir Writing group and to Donna Schilling and Elizabeth Preston for their critiques and encouragement; to Kathy McQuinn, Terry Bronniche, Debbie Ager, and Fred Love for their help with particulars; and to Dr. Rod Krueger for his support of this book. I thank Paulette Bates Alden, Jim Shea, my daughter Christine Aas Larson, daughter-in-law Marcia Aas, and son Peter Aas for their valuable feedback. Thanks to my husband Johannes Aas for his support and patience.

Made in the USA
Lexington, KY
05 November 2013